I Can't Breathe and Other Essays:

Confronting Cognitive Dissonance

Zvikomborero Kapuya

Mwanaka Media and Publishing Pvt Ltd,
Chitungwiza, Zimbabwe
*

Creativity, Wisdom, and Beauty

Publisher: *Mmap*
Mwanaka Media and Publishing Pvt Ltd
24 Svosve Road, Zengeza 1
Chitungwiza, Zimbabwe
mwanaka@yahoo.com
mwanaka13@gmail.com
https://www.mmapublishing.org
www.africanbookscollective.com/publishers/mwanaka-media-and-publishing
https://facebook.com/MwanakaMediaAndPublishing/

Distributed in and outside N. America by African Books Collective
orders@africanbookscollective.com
www.africanbookscollective.com

ISBN: 978-1-77933-149-6
EAN: 9781779331496

© Zvikomborero Kapuya 2024

Acknowledgements

My passion is to tell the world the truth. I believe I am the voice of the voiceless, I speak for the marginalised. I would like to acknowledge the Almighty God, who created me for this purpose, to tell the world the truth about the possibility of a peaceful world and the strong passion for humanity. My gratitude to my late parents Patrick Kapuya and Caroline Chitsinde, joined the ancestors' decades ago, their love and images are cherished. Tears may dry, but memories never fade, I wrote this book clinged to memory of my parents. I would like to acknowledge my family, my guardian parents, Chrispen Kapuya and Desderia Gororo, my siblings for motivating me to pursue this intellectual journey. Without forgetting the woman who is always there for me, a story teller and organic intellectual, my grandmother Juliana Kapuya for being a pillar of strength and source of motivation, I wish her long life.

My gratitude to my former classmates Cynthia Kanyandu, Wadzanai Musangwe, Rudo Mamvura, Tongai Fergus Moyo, Samantha Bako, Nonjabulo Puthi, Tafadzwa Kawonde, Anotida Makotore and Simbarashe Chikomo, there are not just classmates or friends but family, for the success of my literary work there are greatly appreciated. My father Dr Pharaoh Joseph Mavhunga, an unapologetic Pan Africanist and educationist I'm honored to be under his tutelage and guidance. Greatest appreciation to my mentor, Dr Alois Chilunjika, Dr AF Chikerema and Dr M Haurovi for social and academic guidances. My gratitude to my brother

Simbarashe Murape, Simbaramwari Tegwe and my brother Farai Mumanyi.

To my friend Donewell Mapungwana, Brendon Kasirisiri, Justice Sibanda, one of the best ghost writers and poets and Lawrence Khupe. I would like to acknowledge Sailas Jakarasi and Reason Dangaiso my friends from Sanyati. Vengesayi family for helping me in my academic career and Nyanga family, and also not to forget to the person who is always there for me, Lorraine Dhave-Kapuya and my lovely daughter Chikomborero Kapuya. Above all I would like to acknowledge my publisher Tendai Rainos Mwanaka, for his help and modernised publishing skills implemented in prioritising author's voice.

Dedications

To my daughter Chikomborero Caroline Kapuya

To my wife Lorraine Dhave-Kapuya

Table of Contents

Acknowledgements

Dedication

Preface

Preface

What If Africa was never colonised, what will be the narratives today, who will be the oppressor to blame and what will be the relations of the black people and the whites? . I am starting to imagine what post-decoloniality world look like, will black people seek revenge, avenge people killed by the white people during slavery, Jim Crow era, Germany and Belgian genocides in Africa, medical genocides of black people, or they will forgive and focus on rebuilding a better black empire? Does it mean the deconstruction of racism and cognitive dissonance will promote peace? All these questions challenged me to write this collections of essays, triggered by the most global attention of the murder of George Floyd by the US Police which led to global movement of black lives matter, why black lives? Why not all lives? The essays are based on questioning the existing global Oder and normative systems on racism and the deconstruction movement against white supremacy. I believe in peace, I believe in global harmony, but to achieve that the world need to deconstruct cognitive dissonance. Cognitive dissonance is a historical amnesia caused by the falsification of history, epistemicide and cultural genocides manifesting in forms of inferiority complex, self-hate, and self-alienation of the black people and the sense of superiority as natural to white race. It manifests in dichotomy, affects both white race and black people, it can be called coloniality of being. Therefore this situation led to racism, exploitations, political nihilism, exploitation of woman, oppression of the margins therefore the need to confront cognitive dissonance. Confronting is

8

the first step, which explain the realisation of the effects of the subjects and then deconstruct it, hence the need to confront and deconstruct cognitive dissonance. But the journey should not end there, but creates the templates of peaceful post-decoloniality.

Zvikomborero Kapuya

Ph.D Peacebuilding Programme Candidate, International Centre for Nonviolence, Durban University of Technology, South Africa

Introduction

I have seen the worst side of humanity, I witness a lot of moral horror where humanity sink in political oblivion. I have read stories of the worst side of humanity whereby some of the crudest activities includes manufacture of diseases to entrenched biological terrorism, slavery, human sacrifices and establishing power/epistemic dominance. This is the tragedy of modern world. Instead of being celebrated as post-world war, the world turned upside down, it is now worse as people fight for dominance, control and recognitions. Others are fighting to control whilst others are resisting those who want to control, at the end of the day a conflict erupts which leaves thousands corpses on the soil of mother earth, buried in mass graves and some even decomposes without being recognised. Some who claimed to be religious fanatics engage in suicide bombing missions as methods of resisting the universalisation of Western Empire, but in the process many innocent people are killed in the name of enforcing human rights, wars fought and sanctioned imposed which traumatise the system of human rights, it become just an allusion. This is the world we are living in, in the tragedy of humanity. Catholic priests sat down at the Council of Nicaea to decide issues of world peace and proposed the implementation of the religious moral bases to the society, informed by the golden rule of love and fear of sin, but the tribulation and tragedies continued. After thirty years war, Protestant-Catholic wars, at the Treaty of Westphalia 1648, peace was sustained for short period. Monarch and class systems exploded in conflicts which were resolved at Congress of Vienna in

1815, but few years later Italian Unification and Prussian wars destabilised the existing tranquility, the Frankfurt Treaty did not help. In 1914-1918 millions of people were killed in European wars culminating in Paris Peace Settlement but the rise of European dictators, communism and dying age of Pax Britannica resulted in other deadly clashes of 1939-1945, and millions lost their lives. San Francisco Conference of 1945 managed to promote lasting peace through the formation of vibrant international institution governing states' relationships and put more emphaises on human security, but Israel-Palestinian Conflict, Korean War, Vietnam War and Cuban Missile crisis paralysed the existing possibility of peace.

The ideological contestations of communism and liberalism. The collapse of Berlin Wall celebrated by Liberal rightists as milestone achievement towards peace and achieved Hegelian dream of 'Last Man', however due to its Eurocentric nature, it failed to hold peace and Russia's rebirth challenged Pax Americana. Fukuyama (1992) was one of the rightist who celebrated the fall of Union Soviet Socialist Republic as milestone achievements towards peace, trade, democracy, human rights and development. However, few years later, the Somalians' wars, Gulf war and terrorist attacks, which proved wrong to Fukuyama thesis. Huntington (1996) put it that way, the new world order is premised on the conflict between states and non-state actors, this was proved by the rise of transnational terrorism organisations such as Al-Qaeda which orchestrated 9/11 attack. Pandemics wreaked havoc to the world. To trace the origins of these lethal issues which imprison the idea of peace, human beings are to blame and occupy the center of discussions, issues of power competitions, material competitions, arms races and the desire to dominate the world. We are the authors of our own tragedies, but we can be masters of our own destiny, it's possible to come together with our own antagonistic views to engage in consensus to remake the global order. We are to blame for this cognitive dissonance, which makes us morons, war mongers, selfish, monsters, greedy and aggressive. Though Thomas Hobbes argued that, human nature is greedy, aggressive and selfish because it transacts to the anarchic environment where life is brutish, nasty and short, making it suppress those human nature, social contract is the solution. Social contract is what is needed today, at the global level to promote the existence of peace. But the main theme of this collection of essays is to diagnosis the problem of world peace and propose solutions, the challenge is cognitive dissonance which affects all races resultant from white supremacy and systematic racism.

To white race, racism turned them into monsters, and they view other races as inferior, and make themselves global beings of which it is far from reality, therefore the belief of universality and superiority of white race. However, people of color also suffer cognitive dissonance imposed to think by the racial institutions as inferior beings, inferior to white race and thus white image is the figure of everything. This global amnesia, today has led to violence and wars, whereby white race claim natural rights of being a universal being hence through education, media, science and politics defends it, but the realisation of the myth of white superiority drive resistances through any means necessary, the clashes of these two races is linked to contemporary crisis and wars. Colonialism, Slavery, coloniality of being, knowledge and power constructs cognitive dissonance. Confronting these issue is prescription to global peace, which rescues white race from misinterpretation of the global society and black race from the imposed thoughts and inferiority. This is done through rewriting African history, decolonising logics and epistemologies and cherishing a global multicultural society, to defend the last cause and promote the existence of lasting peace in global cosmogony.

Organisation of the Book

The murder of Gorge Floyd by the U.S Police informs themes of this study; racism, colonialism, neo-colonialism and coloniality, discussed and broadened as to make solutions practical to the issue of global peace. Most pacifist scholars believe in the existence of democracy and developments as sources of peace, but this is not necessarily true, to achieve peace they is need to decolonize it, through dismantling racism, global class system, sexism and coloniality. This work is divided into several chapters. This book is a collection of essays, most of the essays explained the same thing but in a different way, the main issue is to broaden the scope of coloniality, cognitive dissonance and wider scale decoloniality movement. It is dedicated to global peace and anti-racisms. The first chapter is a response of the death of George Floyd under the knee of Police Officer Derick Chovin, reflects black and white conflicts in the USA and world at large. The first chapter used "I can't breathe" as symbol for crying for justice for hundreds of years of colonialism, slavery, racial brutality, coloniality and exploitation of the people of color. Today, USA is the last knight guarding the throne of white supremacy and people of color are under the knee of white race, crying I can't breathe, a cry for justice, freedom and equality. The chapter is titled "I can't breathe: The last Knight at the throne of White supremacy". In continuation of the argument

13

in the first essay, the second essay present human issues and activism in the name of black lives matter, its evolutions and impacts to global justice and peace. Why Black lives matter? Why not all lives? What it means to say black lives? Black life or Black lives? All these questions are presented in essay two as to broaden the epistemological scope of human rights and anti-racism as antidote to global peace crisis. The essay is titled "Black Lives Matter: Anti-Racist Campaigns in Modern Times". To comprehend the cognitive dissonance, the discourse of the 'other' presented in third essay as historically constructed identity, through falsification of history, epistemicide, cultural genocides and decoloniality of being. The main important aspect of this essay is, its objective sense is shown on the presentation of the arguments of the effects of cognitive dissonance to white race and people of color, the historical amnesia and the struggle for superiority and expressions of inferiority is what defines the other, therefore not only black race need to deconstruct or decolonizing the mind, but even the white people to be liberated from that historical amnesia planted by their ancestors five centuries ago. The essay is titled "Making the 'Other': The Lost-Self in Global Space". Broadening the discourse of cognitive dissonance as the reason for the existence of paranoid human beings, anti-Semitism holocaust is a good example of the manifestation of cognitive dissonance. Wars, pandemics (HIV/AIDS, Ebola, COVID-19, and Cholera), cultural dispossessions and ethnic wars are a manifestation of cognitive dissonance, but mainly western-made as to maintain the existence of white supremacy, the essay manage to give an adequate explanation of the modern holocaust against the people of color. The essay is titled "21st century Holocaust: Contemporary

Genocides of People of Color". The next essay questions the outcome of Rhodes Must Fall movement of 2015, demanding the removal of Cecil John Rhodes Statue at the University of Cape Town (UCT) and decolonising the curriculum. This is the most popular issue in student activism and academics, whereby the global south universities demands the decolonising of the curriculum to promote critical thinking and restricting the cultural interpretation of the epistemologies. The essay is titled "After Rhodes Must Fall: Student Activism in Confronting Cognitive Dissonance", explains the role of student activism and the black consciousness ideology in decolonising the westernised curriculum. The experiences of black woman in this capitalist world with racialised systems and the reflections of life in ethnic wars, war on terror, knowledge making and epidemics. The essay is titled "Woman of Color in men-made 21st Century: Human liberation". Afrocentric tools of analysis adopted to explain the aspect of feminism in black and African perspective, beyond racism, capitalism and epistemicide. The increase in debate about terrorism and Islamism is an important aspect in analysing the concept of racism, cognitive dissonance and resisting universalism. After 9/11 attack, terrorism used synonymously with Islamism, whereby the Islamist militants Al-Qaeda led by Osama Ben Laden bombed pentagon and twin towers which shock the world and American security. Therefore, Islamist insurgency are now regarded as terrorist, but lack of the definition of terrorism spare them and led to a conclusion that, there are freedom fighters implementing their mission with genuine grievances and resisting Pan Americana. The essay is titled "Islamophobia and Islamic Freedom Fighters: Anti-Racism Perspective in Islamism". Bob Marley, Peter Tosh and

Burney Wailers criticised racism, white supremacy, colonialism, apartheid and slavery through music, inspired liberation movements of the black people across the world and spreads the words of social justice and peace. Bob Marley was an unapologetic Pan Africanist qualified as freedom fighter due to his music and lyrical content which criticised the coloniality global order. The essay "Anti-colonial Legacy of Bob Marley: Decolonial Singing in Reggae Music" explained the life of Bob Marley as Pan Africanist, Afrocentric, decolonialist, revolutionary and the relevance of his music to the people of the south in the contemporary world. From the ghetto, thuggish life style from the unemployed black people, segregated people, they find the way of escape through art, music and intellectual debates. Harlem Renaissance in New York Ghetto is one of the remembered black intellectual movement which gave birth to the idea of Pan Africanism in diaspora, black nationalism and rewriting African History in African perspectives, apart from these results, after civil rights movements, hip-hop activism begin to tell the story of oppression, racism and the black conditions in ghetto through music as to influence policy making based on equality. Tupac Shakur is one of the remembered hip-hop artist who criticised the existing systems through music, the essay is titled "Hip-Hop and Harlem Renaissance: Revolutionary Mentality from Ghetto Voices". The next essay is titled "Wakanda: Filming African Images" based on the Wakandan state image, which is purely African, urban setting, state model, governance, religion, architecture and resources. It is portrayal of the image of Africa untouched to colonialism and slavery, what it should be today and the story is more real. The increase of black people in influential positions such as Barak Obama at US Presidency and Kofi Anan at

United Nations Secretary General, black people in sports and entertainments, this is presented in the essay "Blackening the Whitenised World". This essay described the de-whitenisation of the world, and the increase in blackening of the world, but at the same time question the meaning of blackening the world, not just as occupation of influential positions but packaged with black ideology. The next essays "Black and Beauty: Reflections of Anti-Imperial Aesthetics, Barrel of Pen and Belonging: Rewriting African History in African Perspectives and Rebranding My Identity: African Being in Post-Traditional Society" explained what it means to be a black person, how do we relate with objects and other people, racial differences, aesthetics, imagination, identity and telling the African story in African perspectives. The next essay titled "No More War: De-colorizing, Decoloniality and Liberation of the Soul in the 21st Century", is unapologetically peace movement, explained the strategic aspects in deconstructing cognitive dissonance to achieve the global peace. At the end, an imaginary journey instituted, travel to the post-decoloniality world and imagine how social relations would be. Many scattered imaginations presented, ranging from hatred, avenge, revenges as well as peace, the essay is titled "Imagining Post-Decoloniality Black Nation".

Chapter 1: I Can't Breathe: The last Knight at the throne of white supremacy

No one can forget slave trade, its difficult to erase the memory of colonialism, king Leopold's holocaust in Congo, Herero genocides in Namibia, Tulsa massacre, assassination of anti-racial leaders and continuous killing of black people by the racial institutions. No one can forget the racial injustices in western courts of laws, sentenced to death black people even if there were innocent, it is difficult to forget the role of western parliaments in legislating laws proclaiming death sentences of black people, even alive, physically, our soul are lynched by the injustices in the legal codes. Yes, we cannot forget these atrocities, even Jews cannot forget the Hitler anti-Semitism or the Japanese about Hiroshima and Nagasaki atomic bombings. It's part of our history, shapes the present generation and our eagerness not just to intergrate but to create a peaceful world, where black and white play together, receive the same trial in the courts of laws, with same prieveledges in public spaces and equal treatment in the global social space. I can't breathe is a cry for justice, justice for the historic injustices, justice for present racial systems and justice for the existing mental slavery. The existentiality of black being in the global space is mostly determined by the coloniality of space, which suffocates potentials, capabilities and psychological functionality of black person as black being. As a black person, I can't breathe because of my skin color, because of my intellectual capabilities, because of my intellectual capabilities connected to the historic legacy of the past, therefore the western knee is on my neck. The atrocious behaviors by the white race resulted from fear of genetic competition with people of color. For Cresswelsing (1991), the logic, thoughts, speeches, attitudes in consolidating white race is founded on fear of genetic annihilation by the people of color and numerical inadequacy.

Being and space are related social realities, whereby space reflects the experiences of being and the relations with objects. Therefore, in this context space is polluted by the racial-crudest logics, crowded with racism symbolic objects, hence suffocates people of color. "I can't breathe", said George Floyd, a plea for help under the knee of Derick Chauvin, a white police officer, he cried, but no one was there to help, even the police. He joined Malcom X, Martin Luther King Junior, Thomas Sankara, Patrice Emery Lumumba and other revolutionaries who at the hand of white supremacy breadth were snatched, silenced by death.

In this essay, I can't breathe is euphemist language to explain the negative effects of racism, colonialism and coloniality of people of color. Not only George Floyd utters these words, but revolutionary figures lynched, beheaded, killed by the white-made diseases, assassinated, deprived their right to life. White supremacy is genocidal, aiming to exterminate what is black in intellectual phenomenon and the bodies of people of color through colonialism, slavery, defacto resurgence of slavery and coloniality of being in contemporary global space. The present global space is polluted by white supremacy, therefore Africa, Asia, and Latin America is yelling, I can't breathe. It is also astonishing to witness the death of black people and degrading inhuman treatment in United States of America under the hands of police who are supposed to protect people's rights despites of color, the country that boasts of human rights, the country claimed to be world police and dedicates its foreign policy to promote human rights. A

19

country claimed an image of modern civilisation happens to kill people because of their color, funds rebel wars in Africa, exploits oil resources in the Middle East and Africa, sanction the innocent people for taking back their ancestral land. U.S.A sanctions Iran for nationalizing its oil resources and Cuba for being an anti-capitalist state. Venezuela was slaped with sanctions and condemned for abusing human rights but the reason behind this was oil, who is to sanction US? Nagasaki and Hiroshima atomic bombs genocides, Tulsa massacre of 1921, slavery, genocides against black people in Africa and biological terrorism. For Chomsky (2016), US is the most terrorist state, terrorise people around the world reflecting white supremacy and furthers its interests of controlling the whole world. It is a new knight guarding the throne of white supremacy.

> "It's uncontroversial that the United States is a leading terrorist. In fact, it's the only state that was condemned for international terrorism by the highest bodies, the international Court of Justice in 1986" (Chomsky 2016)

It was condemned in 1986, and still continue to terrorise the global societies around the world. Chomsky (2016) opines that, "the US imposed sanctions on Iran, killed more people than Weapons of Mass Destruction in Iraq and the rest of Middle East". Therefore, the behavior of the United States in global politics is a symbolic gestures of the response of white race from self-alienation. It is above all the international bodies, because no state can dare to sanction U.S besides Russia and China (Amin 2010), white supremacy is the worst enemy of humanity, anti-Semitism, slavery, colonialism and epidemic holocaust happened as a result of white supremacy. Cresswelsing (1991) concurs that, if scholars ignore the white supremacy in studying global anti-humanity events and behaviors, the theory or arguments will be superficial, far from reality.

> "The carnage wrought by western, ostensibly Christian leaders over the last six decades- including a word war and cold war, a holocaust, two atomic bombs, repression of wars of independence, then fuelling of proxy wars, nuclear brinksmanship, and the support of dictators and state and non-state terrorists- makes it spurious to view Islam as a more inherently violent religion or civilisation" (Rama Mani)

White supremacy is the source of violence, not Islam as they claim. It is responding from the existence of white supremacy or systematic racism. All these wars fought resulted from the logic, actions, speeches and behaviors of white race to compensate them from self-alienation. US is the global monster, roars to spread fear to the opponents of the system. This essay presents intellectual thoughts, there is need to navigate on the high seas of post-positivist theories of political and social relations.

> "White supremacy is an active political system in our nation, it promotes and perpetuates racial discrimination and racist violence. Consequently black people must remain aware and vigilant every day in our lives whether confronting people of color who have internalized racism or in all white settings where it is likely that many of those present have not unlearned racism" (Hook 2009: 89)

Racism as a political theory is synonymously defined as white supremacy, resulting from the phobia of genetic annihilation and selfish behavior of white race to dominate people of color. It is based on racial segregation in education, law, politics, media and dehumanisation of people of color, putting them into ghettos, prisons and prisoning the minds in white controlled education. Instead of calling courts, schools, churches and prisons as place of learning, correction and worship, it become the cultic centres for nourishing white supremacy. Hook (2009) justifies the political issues of racism's influences on the psychological and social behavioral responses between white race and people of color. The former act as the main factor agency in the implementation of white supremacy and the latter as the victims. Therefore, black people must continue to threaten this political system through unlearning black inferiority and social activists should claim the glorious destiny of the people of color and promote peace.

Post-structural theory provides intellectual thoughts on the relation of self (white race) and other (people of color) (Butler 1991 and Foucault 1967) and its hierarchy manifestations and power projections. That hierarchy relations is what is discussed here as white supremacy and sustained by the methodology of meta-narratives, controlled by the West to globalize the perspective of the inferiority of people of color and superiority of white race. Therefore, the existing narrative which romanticise the western civilisation as the fundamental discourse to social construction of power. Though the theory also source its intellectual exposition from Eurocentric scholarship, it manages to give an adequate explanation in understanding the results of interracial interactions, white race (self) and people of color (other). White race claimed the title of global self through the existing narratives disqualifying people of color and give the title 'self' to other as a result of their non-existence in global civilisation. However, Transmodenity came into being to give a subverse analysis of racism as a global problem which manifests in epistemicide, linguisticides and cultural genocides of the people of color (Grosfoguel 2007, Mignolo 2013, Dussel 1977, Wynter 2010). Afrocentric intellectual thoughts based on the analytical consciousness of adopting African agency in analysing blackness and racism is important in understanding of the discourse, I can't breathe, it acts as a solution to unlearn racist epistemologies, and remember the dismembered. Asante (2006) defines Afrocentric as a paradigm that seeks to examine every aspect of subject place of Africans in historical, literary, philosophical, architectural and moral life of the Africans.

These theories are critical in the development of the discourse, I can't breathe, hence at this moment let us go through the historical journey and analyse the events which suffocates people of color, snatched breadth from their nostrils and how there are relegated to the periphery. The famous Valladolid judgment consolidates white supremacy in global space. It is one of the classical debates in the history of human rights, colonialism and slavery. The main subject of the debate was the treatment of indigenous people (Native Americans) by the conquerors, justifications of the conquest of America, the relation between the settler and Amerindians and christianisation of the native of the New World. The debate held in 1550-51 in Celago de San Gregorio in the Spanish city of Valladolid (Minahane 2014 and Ludwig 2001). The debate was between Bishop of Chipas, father Bartolome de La Casas and the humanist Juan Gines de Sepulveda. Barlome de La Casas argued from theological moral perspective, premised on the writings of Saint Augustine, arguing that though Indians practices of human sacrifices and cannibalism, it not enough to qualify them as barbarians using Aristotlean logic, they deserve better treatment,

23

respect and be treated as human beings equal to the colonisers (Grosfoguel 2013). However , Juan Gines de Sepulveda criticised this stand point, and argued that, human sacrifices, cannibalism and primitive mentality qualifies the Amerindians to Barbarians, as according to Aristotle- a people without soul, without intelligentsia and behaving as animals. Therefore he proposed that, this must be stopped through enslavement, conversion to Catholicism and conquest. In regard to that, the debate remained stalemate, however King Philip II used Bartolome de La Casas arguments to create laws and integrated Amerindians into Spanish nation. Therefore, hunting the barbarians was another struggle. This event is significant in the history of black suffocation by the imperialist, since the Aristotlean concept of barbarism was applied to Africans, as people without history, without soul, without intelligentsia, cruel, primitive, barbarians and inhuman.

> "Homo peli nigre, was the name given to a variety of the human species who are entirely black and are found in the torrid zones, especially in that part of Africa which lies within the tropics. In the complexion of negroes we meet with various shades, but they likewise differ from other men in all the features of their face, with round check, high cheek-bones, a forehead somewhat elevated, a short, broad, flat nose, thick lips, small ears, ugliness and irregularities in shape, characterises their external appearance. The Negro women have loins greatly depressed, and very large buttocks, which gave back the shape of saddle. Vices, the most notorious seem to be the portion of this unhappy race, idleness, treachery, revenge, cruelty, impudence, stealing, lying, profanity, debauchery, nastiness and intemperance are said to have extinguished the principles of

natural law, and to have silenced the reproofs of conscience. They are strangers to every sentiment of confession, and are awful example of corruption of man when left to himself' (Encyclopedia Britannica 1798)

Therefore, that was the description of the black people or Negroes as less human beings. This was written by an outsider, from an outsider perspectives with little understanding of the Africans which distorts the image for hundreds of years. This outside perspective reflects Eurocentric paradigm, based on biased interpretation of black cosmology and it led to the removal of Negroes in intelligentsia. This basic interpretation of Negro race ushers in the contemporary view of Africans by the white race and have psychological impacts to the victims, embracing the inferiority complex and justified scientific arrangement of the society. The above description of the Negroes, informed by the writings of Juan Gines de Sepulveda of justifying slavery and colonialism as mission civilistrice. There is a strong argument here, who was a barbarian then, one who opines slavery, colonialism and mistreatment of other equal human beings and the one who establish peaceful states governed by cultural values? It is prudent to argue that, colonialism and slavery was the most barbaric act in human history, manifests in forced labor, shipping of millions of Africans from Africa to America as slaves, culturally dislocates the native, ill-treatment, violent land dispossession and genocides. That was the most barbaric behavior whereby black people cried I can't breathe, in the slave ships, in the white plantations, under ruthless colonial regimes but singing songs to re-awaken their spirit and sourcing air to breathe again.

Therefore the barbaric sentiments of black people, described by Hegel and Pritchard, justified the enslavement of people of color. Today, Europe and America is ahead of Africa in terms of infrastructure development resulted from the use of cheap labor and forced labor from African slaves. The film 12 years slave and Django Unchained depicts the reflections of experiences of black people during slavery, treated as non-humans; branded, handcuffed, tortured, racially segregated and auctioned as objects. Slave owners become property owners through huge profits from slavery business, built empires and corporations. Fredrich Douglass narrates slave experiences in "Narrative of the Life of Fredrich Douglass", an American slave explained his life story; born as slave and the challenges faced by being a slave in white supremacy environment. Slavery was also a response to self-alienation and self-hate of the white race, threatened by the existence of people of color. The action was more pernicious and extreme, but served the purpose of consolidating white supremacy.

The master-slave relations was the historic power construction, based on introducing the racial or societal structure characterised by class system, white (master, aristocracts) as superior and blacks as inferior. White superiority funded by materialism and owned black people; black people were not workers but slaves, forced to work without the implementation of workers' rights, no morals, legal codes or court of law to speak their rights. That was another sad part of slavery, wicked and barbaric treatment of black people by the whites in the contemporary world, master-slave relations illuminates in racism and policies envisioning segregation (Cresswelsing 1991, Clarke 1998, Joachanan 2002). Negroes were ill-treated by the slave masters and stripped of their dignity. This is

26

related to the present issues, the killing of black people who resist or protest against the system.

After the abolishment of slavery, another pathetic, barbaric, deceitful and cruel strategy against the black people was launched in form of colonialism. Europeans set down at the Berlin Conferences in 1884, decided the future of Africa as extension of European empire. Northern and some parts of West Africa given to France, Britain acquired large territories from all corners of Africa as a result of Cecil John Rhodes colonial ambitions of Cape to Cairo, Belgium was given heart of Africa (Congo), Tanganyika, Zanzibar, Namibia were given to Germany and Portugal also occupied coastal areas and Islands. The main theme of Berlin Conference was to settle the territorial expansion disputes among Europeans and explain the conditions of conquest, boundaries, and the whites and natives relations. No African representatives was there. To consolidate conquest, cultural demonization, divide and rule, military conquest and land occupation was also effected. This scenario reduced Africans into ghettos and reserves, forced labor initiatives were launched. France used the policy of assimilation which problematises the African identities, victimized from being self to emulate and imitate French cultures. The knee was heavy to Africans, the glorious African states, cosmologies, social relations and customary systems were suffocated, under heavy knee of European colonisers. Africa pleaded, I can't breathe.

In an attempt to find air to breathe, Africans launched anti-colonial resistance but were unsuccessful, outweighed by the European guns which resulted in the massacre of black people. Anti-colonial resistance leaders were hanged. Mbuya Nehanda famously known for "my bones will rise" (mafupa angu achamuka) and other leaders of anti-colonial resistance were hanged by whites. The reason was to spread fear to any colonial resistance, it was the most atrocious behavior of the people who claimed to come to Africa to civilize black people. King Leopold killed millions of Congolese, Germany genocides of the Herero tribe left a permanent mark to the Africans in Namibia and the whole continent. African nationalist prisoned, detained and killed. In South Africa, Nelson Mandela was imprisoned for 27 years, Steve Biko was assassinated and Solomon Mahlangu among others murdered. No one can forget the ruthless massacre of South African students by the Apartheid police on 16 June 1977. That was the cruelest side of white supremacy, when it feel threatened, it always responded aggressively.

After world war 1, black soldiers came from war with high hopes of freedom at home but the situation remained worse, Jim Crow laws and lynching of black people become a legal mass slaughter of black man. Black people built 'Black Wall Street" in Tulsa, the wealthiest black community in history of African Americans, they built churches, schools, hospitals and corporations. The increase in black wealth threatened white supremacy, hence they accused an innocent black person of rape, white people demanded justice, and justice was lynching. Black people decided to stand on moral grounds, defended the innocent black person but in confrontations the exchange of fire begin, the government send armed police to back up the white people and Black Wall Street was destroyed to ground, people lost their homes and thousands of black people killed. This was the most racial act in the American history. Threatening white supremacy, means treason and the sentence is death.

To people of African descent, lynched and killed by the white people, resisting white supremacy was equivalent to treason. Afro-Americans were sentenced to death before even committing crimes. Black people are the most unemployed people in the USA and ghetto residence conditions influences the existence of 'black being', as criminals, teen mothers, drug addicts, homosexuals, prostitutes/strippers. Homicides, femicides, single parenting and divorces reflects the conditions of blacks in the USA. These behaviors are not innate or natural, but influenced by the environment crowded with white supremacist systems which snatch the humanity of blacks. Black people are referred to as non-humans in the white sociological schema justifying this with the reflective experiences of black ghettos as the hot spot of drug trafficking, homicides and crimes. It's a psychological manifestations of the victims of racism.

The period of civil rights movement and the present events are much similar. The anti-racism resistance leaders murdered, imprisoned and assassinated by the white race seeks to defend the system. White supremacy is built with blood, sorrows and sweats of people of color. Martin Luther King Junior and Malcom X advocates for the rights of black people, social equality, social justice and end of the impunity of racism, which basically mean the popular demand of the dismantling of white supremacy. The realisation of the mental slavery, the consciousness of oppression builds the human desire of autonomy and liberation among black people to enjoy the natural rights. Malcom X murdered, Martin Luther murdered, Patrice Emery Lumumba, Thomas Sankara and Samora Machel assassinated, were deemed threats to the capitalist world order. It takes me back to Obert Nyathi song 'senzen'ina', it sorrowfully explains the pain of black people and the white dominated world and questions the reasons for this treatment.

In the politics of resources in post-colonial Africa, Europeans continue to exploit resources, leaving the whole continent poor. I can't breathe, I can't breathe, so said George Floyd, a symbolic expression of black people suffering in the past and present, continuing to suffer under the knee of white supremacy. I can't breathe, he closed his eyes for good and joined ancestors.

Chapter 2

Black Lives Matter: Anti-Racist Campaigns in Modern Times

Why black lives matter? Why not all lives? Black life or black lives? These questions developed an epistemic domain of the concept and aspect. The most chanted slogan of the 21 Century, *Black Lives Matter*. After the centuries of atrocious and perilous mass slaughters of blacks. Anti-white supremacist and anti-colonial demonstrations across the globe seek justice against the westernised unjust political systems. The murder of Floyd George in Minneapolis incite the existence of serious global movements against the injustices launched to people of color. He was murdered by the Police Officer in a broad day light, chocked by knee and yelling I can't breathe till he died. It's not the first time US Police did that to black people, of course they want to promote justice and arrest criminals but the horrible killing of black people makes one to think otherwise. Maybe the US Police Institution is designed to target Afro-American and people of color, like the World Judicial systems, International Criminal Court (ICC) prosecutes only Africans but there are war criminals in the US and Europe, which transcribe to the notion that ICC only targets Africans (Mude 2017). Therefore, it is worth to argue that, the global systems are designed to annihilate Africans and people of color as a threat in genetic competition. The Cress Theory of Color Confrontation prove it right, since self-alienation and the fear of numerical inadequacy resulted in anti-black holocaust as psychological compensatory methods and exterminates the threat on the way.

It is astonishing that, everyday, Black people are killed by Police Officers in broad day light, not only in the United States, but also in the United Kingdom, Germany and other European countries, and most of these killings are race related. Why this enmity? This aggressiveness which even devour the existence of human dignity, why these war against defenseless blacks? Cress Welsing (1991) argued that fear of the genetic annihilation and numerical inadequacy has resulted in logic thoughts, speeches and actions directed towards compensating white race from the psychological feeling of self-alienation. The notion is psychological. Therefore, the anger directed towards black people though in an atrocious way, the western world values the outcome it illuminates as preservation of white supremacism. White supremacism, the synonym of racism need to survive therefore it needs military, social, economic and political expedition, If it fails to survive or is threatened it means the end of white superiority in global space therefore the revolution against it is dangerous but needs lion hearted courage among the people of color.

I wrote this essay in response to the tragic death of Floyd George under the knee of Police Officer. The war is racial, the killing was based on race system. Whereby Floyd George represents people of color and Derek Chauvin, the Police Officer, represents white race, it goes back to Hitter Anti-Semitism policy in Germany and Namibia, whereby people of color were murdered as the logic to maintain the Aryan origin of Germany. Why Black people were forced to leave their homes and be enslaved in America centuries ago? After slavery, blacks faced segregation in Apartheid South Africa, Racism in USA and colonialism, and now the police continues to murder and imprison black people, It means black people are the most enemy of the white race, If there are enemy, black people responds defenselessly and are willing to live together with the white race. Blacks are the one who build New York economy, but today they are murdered in broad day light. This paper is not aimed to incite racism, but navigate on the objectives sense of social realities against the people of color and white race relations in the contemporary world.

> "It felt personal. As I watched the breadth ebb out of George Floyd under the deliberate weight knee of the uniformed white police officer on his neck, I felt the Asphyxia myself. That human being struggling for breadth on the street on Minneapolis could have been me, could have been one of my cousins, my nephews, my nieces, my school mates, or their children, could have been their children who live in United Sates of America" (Elizabeth Ohene 2020. I can't Breathe Here)

This script, written by Ghanaians, who felt threatened by the white supremacism, who felt the wound of the Black Family, a dark cloud continues to shadow the black race as a family, daily or annually these cases continue to happen. Malcom X and Martin Luther King Assassinated as the project of anti-black power movement. In Africa, leaders speak against the white supremacy were assassinated and removed by military coup allegedly sponsored by the Western Capitalist/ white race. For example anti-colonial and revolutionary leaders such as Amilcar Cabral, Samora Machel, Patrice Emery Lumumba, Thomas Sankara and many others. Africa was robbed of her greatest leaders by the imperialist, the agenda was to stop decolonial and anti-colonial movements in Africa, since it awakened black consciousness a threat to the European order. These sponsored coups and assassinations were meant to destabilise the rise of Black empire as powerful or superpower in

33

global politics. Therefore, Africa is the home of many people of color, so if the real independence meant the rise of the continent, it translated as the potential threat against the white race, hence the strategy is to keep them under the yoke of domination, coloniality and conforms to the systems of white supremacy.

Africa is a family, values Ubuntu cosmology "I am because we are", hence the death of these anti-colonial revolutionary statesman and the Afro-American anti-racist leaders means a loss to the Black Family, robbed of their geniuses by the global capitalist. Many black people during American Civil war of 18th century, First World War, Second World War and Vietnam War were on the forefront of the battle, fought bravely for the white race and died in the battlefields. That was another mechanism to deal with the people of color, since the killing of people of color is the final order to exterminate the potential threat to white supremacism. Man are the most targeted, imprisoned, killed and castrated in the history of Afro-American and African colonial history, and to date man are the main target, the main reason is to cause confusion on black nationalism, remove the images of Father figure in political theatre to loosen the steering of revolution and future anti-white supremacist movements. However, the fortunate part is African and people of color are spiritually consciousness, they seek to re-dig the archives and read the history of these great people to energize the struggle.

I can't breathe is symbolic to the expression of the life of Afro-Americans in United States and Africans around the globe. The global order suffocates the livelihoods of people of color, marginalised to the ghetto, marginalised to global periphery, alienated from global decision making, their life is meaningless, there is no air or oxygen to breathe, perhaps carbons are there to breath which immediately kill the hopes of life of the people of color.

Black Lives Matter, an anti-racism movement formed to fight against racial injustices in the US and the globe at large source its strength from the genetic supremacy of melanin, the great African History (Egyptian Civilisation and other Great African Civilisations), black contribution in modern civilisation and the historical wars of resistance (Haiti Revolution. Anti-racism movement by Black Panther Party and the historical existence of anti-white supremacy fathers figures (Malcom X and Martin Luther King Junior) provides fertile grounds for anti-racism campaigns to blossom. These are the sources of strength and molds the ideology of black power or Black Nationalism aimed at rebutting the black inferiority in global space, and self-liberation from the complex white supremacist structures and create a strong Black nation beyond geopolitical locations. Black Lives Matter formulated on the problem of historic slave trade, colonialism and contemporary racism, social activism and intellectual movements is the strategy premised on black power, Afrocentric and Pan African Ideology aimed to create social justices among races. Black lives Matter not only in United States but across the world is response or reaction to increased murder, killing and imprisonment of the people of color in the United States and Europe whereby the idea is consolidating white supremacy. The mass murder of the Arabs by the United States in the so called 'war on terror' one day will led to the Campaign, "Arab lives Matter", the death of Iranian General and millions of Iran people due to sanctions imposed by the West build a serious movement against the West. Japan is silent about Hiroshima and Nagasaki Atomic Bombings but there are organisations in japan who are willing to campaign against the US, on Japanese Lives Matter. If the world rise against the white race, it will be the end of racism or perhaps beginning of another, but the point here is, racism remain the most primitive behavior in the 21st century. Blacks Lives Matter is now a global movements concerned about the lives of marginalised black people in New Zealand (Maori and Aborigines as people of color), blacks in South East Asia, Blacks in USA, Europe, Caribbean and Africa.

Chapter 3

Making the 'Other': The lost-self in Global Space

The challenge of the 21st Century is believed to be terrorism, climate change, dictatorship, nuclearism, epidemics, natural disasters and cyber-terrorism but this essay deviates attention from these phenomenon and focuses on the problem of lost-self, which is psychological and resulted in the creation of the 'other'. Who is this self? How did he/she lost self? And why it matters? These philosophical abstractions engages in the epistemic development of this particular projections. The psychology of self in global is based on the philosophy of existentialism, whereby this 'lost' is more of psychological, metaphysical than physical. This self is African, people of color; she/he is the bottom of everything in global space, in the margins of global civilisation, him /her in the periphery of global decisions. Then how did it happen? It did not happen accidentally or coincidentally, but informed by the systematic constructions of the global space by the white race. This essay is not a racist incitation, but aimed at exposing the objective stance of Africans as people of color and how they relate with the outside word in the westernised modernity.

The world as cognitive space has no place for Africans, since the system designed to dominates people of color is compensatory psychology. To understand the concept of compensatory psychology, it is prudent to revisit Dr Frances Cress Welsing Thesis

> "The color-confrontation theory states that the white or color-deficient Europeans responded psychologically, with a profound sense of numerical inadequacy and color inferiority in their confrontations with the world's people-

37

all of whom possessed varying degrees of color-producing capacity. This psychological response, whether conscious or unconscious revolved on inadequacy on the most obvious and fundamental part of their being, their external appearance. As might be anticipated in terms of psychological theories, whites defensively developed an uncontrollable sense of hostility and aggression. This attitude has continued to manifest itself throughout the history of mass confrontations between whites and people of color. That initial hostility and aggression come only from whites, is record in innumerable diaries, journals and books written by whites. Also records indicates that only after a long period of great abuse have non-whites responded defensively with any form of counter-attack. This perplexing psychological reaction of whites has directed towards all people with the capacity to produce melanin. However, the most profound aggressions have been directed towards black people, who have the greatest color potential and therefore, are the most envied and feared in genetic color competition" (Cress Welsing 1991:4-5)

Color confrontations discourses remain true in searching the manufacturing of the 'other' or the lost-self in global space. From Cress Welsing theory, self-hate, self-alienation, fear of numerical and color inadequacy among the white people influence aggressive behavior towards people of color fearing black people ability to produce color, knowledge and survival in different climatic conditions, therefore black people in the world threatens the existence of white people as race. She went on to discuss the issue of black male sexual organs carrying color genes, happens to be the threat of white race. Which means white females wishes to have

38

black babies, and black males as the first priority of mating. That is the reason why black people were lynched and castrated in United States of America (USA). In doing so, white people compensate themselves through racism as political and psychological system. This was done through colonising the image of God, symbols, inferiorization of blacks, epistemicide and holocaust against the blacks and all people of color. Therefore, Cress Theory of Color Confrontations played a most important role in understanding the social realities of racism, hatred against the black people and subjugations of the people of color in the global space.

In this regard, post-structural theorist such as Marx Althuser, Michael Foucault, Judith Butler and Jacques Derrida made it clear that 'people's freedoms are limited by the existence of social and political systems designed to control human behavior, such as government, morals, laws and cosmologies. These institutions exist after society agreed consciously and unconsciously to have them as anti-thesis of state of nature. But the challenge is all about these cultural solutions to maintain the greater good of the society are westernised, captured in the snares of coloniality as psychological compensatory discourses to counter genetic color confrontation, knowledges, ontology and cosmologies. Therefore, because of the defenseless resistance of people of color (Blacks), marginalised to the periphery out of the system they did not create. Democracy, human rights and neo-liberalism are not created for Africans or Blacks to benefit from, but for white people to dominate the global sphere to counter the genetic color competition.

This essay, depends on Cress-Welsing arguments on racism and the psychological manifestation of it, it is also aimed at exploring the methods used by the whites to create the 'other' as psychological being or lost-self in global space. Prior to the exploration of the methodological frameworks employed by this so called white race to fed white supremacy, there is need to define who the other is? Who is the lost-self talked about? Of course Dr. Frances Cress Welsing thesis and Edward Said identifies the other as Indians, Mongolians, Africans, Semites and Arabs. In the book "Phenomenology of Decolonizing the University: Contemporary Thoughts in Afrikology", I defined 'the other' as psychological being who has lost his/her identity as a result of colonialism and complex coloniality, who is no longer original self (African) and not even the person he/she emulates, hence the other. An identity less, cultureless and empty being. At this moment, the other is defined as the victims (individuals or groups) of white supremacist, psychological, lost their original self-referring to white race traumatised by the system to believe in black inferiority and the people of color. Therefore, the other is not only the people of color, but even contemporary white race, needs self-evaluation to get back to the real sense of humanity and escape from this mental delusional image planted by their ancestors. In precise, the other is a being (white and people of color) victimized by the systems of white supremacy, stripped away their senses of humanity and influenced by negative behaviors (white and people of color race) to behave in racial inferiority/superiority,

Epistemicide: According to Ndhlovu-Gatsheni (2013), epistemicide is a cultural genocide launched by the white people to dominate the cognitive empire and kill non-western bodies of knowledge.

"The epistemic strategy has been crucial for western global designs. By hiding the location of the subject of enunciation, European/Euro-American colonial expansions and dominations, create hierarchy of superior and inferior knowledge, and thus superior and inferior people around the world" (Grosfoguel 2007:1)

The creation of hierarchy of knowledge was designed on geopolitical location of people of color and the psychology of compensation. Fearing people of color, their knowledge as a source of pride inferiorised and relegated to the bottom in global economy of knowledge. This happened after Immanuel Kant thesis of 'Anthropology in Pragmatic Point of View', whereby the Nordic Peninsula was redrawn as the center of global knowledge, Iberian Peninsula and the rest of the world disqualified as centers of knowledge, that is the reason why the countries first known for European Voyages and colonialism, there is the non-existence of Portugal and Spain in mainstream theories of social realities. This happened after the fall of Grenada in 1492 whereby the knowledge in the Iberian Peninsula was treated with contempt, as a result of Spanish and Portuguese philosophers who were educated by the African. Carthage was the intellectual heritage of Luso-Hispanic world. Also, the Nordic Peninsula claimed Greek heritage of Knowledge, since the finest scholars of Athens, Democritus, Hypocrates, Pythagoras, Thucydides, Socrates, Plato and the famous Aristotle ignites the existence of western scholarship. Theories propounded by western philosophers, scientist and social scientist source foundation from Greek cosmogony (Diop 1974). However, for a surprise those Greek philosophers were schooled by the Egyptians, black Egyptians in Africa and even stole written literature by the African forefathers. The complete version of this issue presented by Cheikh Anta Diop (1974) in *African Origins of Civilisations: Myth or Reality* and George James (1954) *Stolen Legacy: Egyptians Origins of Greek Philosophy*. Therefore, the existence of African great scholarship and genetic inheritance of color, threatens the ontological existence of white race consciously and unconsciously, therefore a plan to plunder these magnificent African stories. White people deny the existence of blacks and world civilisation, Egypt is relocated to Mediterranean civilisation, whitened and we people of color removed from the great history. Fredrich Hegel declared that, Africans are people without history, without sense and without soul". This was obvious that this aggressive insult was from the self-alienated being, psychological fear of the numerical inadequacy, deficiency of melanin and intellectual incapacity, therefore the westernised social historiography premised on this particular perspective.

Africa was dubbed 'A Dark Continent', a way to vulgarize the word dark (color), use it as a synonym of emptiness, non-existence of history and civilisation. This aggressive display universalised in academics and indeed consume the confidence and pride of 'blacks in the world'. This invites Manganyi (1974) presentation of 'being black in the world', which contributed immensely to the psychological reflective meaning of being a person of color in westernised universe, bear images such as non-intelligence, primitive, barbaric, and non-proficiency. Not to forget Dambudzo Marechera (1979) stated that, "I became an outsider in my own country, my own history", "all these years I tried to make a skeleton of myself in my own cupboard". The reflective experience of Black people in "House of Hunger" and "Black Insider", explained how the black people relates with white people, and their systems influenced by the inferiority-superiority capitalistic social structure in westernised universe. It is studied that, only five countries dominates the social sciences, humanities and physical sciences theories, namely France, German, United Sates of America, Italy and Britain, it is not a mere hypothesis but a proved scientific fact (Grosfoguel 2007). And the knowledge is patriarchal to compensate white males from the self-alienation.

Demonisation of Cultures: Lezra (2010) argued that, demonising was the best strategy used by the west to consolidate white supremacy. This was done through trans-atlantic slave trade and colonialism. As a result of Valladolid Judgment, 'Indians were not spared from being people without soul and were transferred to Africans", it authorizes the need to fill the empty gap, the non-existence of soul in black being with white Christianity, White Image of God and the opposite of black image as symbolic meaning of devil. Black people were the most spiritual people, but European missionaries through mission civilistrice converted Africans to Christianity, using Biblical passages to justify slavery and colonialism. The use of totems, African cultures and rituals were demonised, replaced by the Christian religion and cultures, and this distorted the existence of African being and lost-self in global space.

For Dussel (1994), "cogito ego sumi", locus preceded by 150 years of European "ego conquitus" (I conquer, therefore I am", the European being universalised, his (patriarchal nature) philosophies declared universal truth. Rene Descartes thought of "I think, therefore I am" demonopolise knowledge from Catholic influence,

God replaced by European Being to consolidate white supremacy. This is done through coloniality of knowledge, from elementary to post-secondary education, the use of European languages as official languages and imitating European being among people of color fed the process of the creation of the 'other'.

Therefore, in questioning the ontological existence of white-self and black-self remain problematic, whereby white people or people of color are people without history, primitive, barbaric, lack scientific mind and inferior beings. This is drilled in each and every generations of white people for half a century, hence they lost-self, lost their truthful being and need to liberate from that mess, taught them the truth behind racism, hatred against the people of color. In modern context, coloniality, democracy, neoliberalism and contemporary cosmogonies creates alienated Black beings from their roots and origins that manifests in form of self-hate. Therefore, the world then is going to continue to tore apart as a result of the existentiality of the 'other', both white race and people of color.

Chapter 4

21st Century Holocaust: Contemporary Genocides of People of Color

The decline of human dignity in modern times oriented from the development of technology and systems of oppressions, not to say technology is bad, but its psychological effects to human beings is the lost-self, lost dignity and increase in apocalyptic behaviors. It is not an anti-technology argument, but exposing its impacts to humanity, though it managed to connect cities, nations and cultures together in global village ever before. The justification of the argument is nuclearism and world wars resulted from the technical competitions, but these issues owed to the return of 'state of nature' where life is short, brutish and nutsy (Hobbes). The ghost of Thomas Hobbes hunt the present generations, there are laws and systems to conquer human behaviors, however aimed to serve the interest of the view, which invites Marxist view of law argued that, laws designed by the capitalist to exploit the proletariat. For instance, United States and Western countries designed International Criminal Court (ICC) through the promulgation of Rome Statue of 1998 to prosecute individual who commits crimes against humanity (genocide, rape, extermination, mass murder), but to date US Generals commits heinous crimes in the Middle East but are walking free, however most convicted persons from this Court are Africans. Therefore, It is regarded as a racial court to serve the interests of the global capitalist (Mude 2018, Blair and Curtis 2009). This is the tragedy of 21st Century, but the main theme of this essay is the dynamics of holocaust against the people of color which originated from self-alienation, self-hate and the fear

45

of color inadequacy against the blacks that resulted in the most cruel responses that threatens the existing thread of humanity.

The theory was explained by Dr. Frances Cress Welsing, but at this juncture, I seek to explain further the conspiracies behind biological warfare as the make-up of the coloniality of global space and a method in strengthening the livelihoods of white supremacist ideology. The happening of Anti-Semites holocaust informs the dynamics of post-world wars mass murder resulting in the existence of deadly diseases such as HIV/AIDS, Ebola and COVID-19 among others to consume the world population, mainly people of color. There are conspiracies behind the existence of these diseases, whereby political scientist believe that there are 'men-made' to serve political interest, but this argument is refuted by the world health governed bodies by being criticised for being non-scientific. However many theories support this political science conspiracy theory. There are men-made, the western man or white males are responsible for the creation of these diseases as compensatory psychology of self-alienation and fear annihilation. There is nothing more about conspiracy, but its objective to argue in relation of the artificial creation of the global pandemics. In comprehending this modern biological warfare and planned mass slaughter against the people of color, there is need to revisits the Hitler Judeophobic discourses that happened between 1933-1954, whereby six million (6,000,000) Jews were murdered. It shock the existence of human dignity, and most scholars research on the topic to understand the reason for this grave hatred, but in a depth analysis, white supremacism surface as the reason for this serious hatred against the Semites. In most cases, the logic of Anti-Semitism in western scholarship is based on strengthening the status quo, defending the white supremacist and are focused on other challenges which are not scientific, here the cause of Anti-Semitism is white supremacy.

Cress-Holocaust theory stresses the point that, the behavior of planned mass slaughter against the Semites as people of color, people of mixed race (whites and blacks) originated from North Africa threatens the genetic existence of 'Aryan' (white race) must be looked as immoral challenges of moral passion in the fundamental principles of humanity. The logic, thought, speech, action, emotional responses and perceptions is of absolute logical necessity for a people who historically have been in fear of genetic annihilation by the people of color. This military responses to the people of color is beyond economic competition or political but based on the fear of genetic competitions, therefore this was a puritanical agenda to purify the German population, as a nation of Aryans only.

> "I was convinced that the 'final solution' for the Semites in Europe was associated with the 'atomic bomb solution' for Japanese people in World War II and that the anti-Semitism of Europe and America was intimately related to apartheid of Southern Africa and historic pattern of treatment (mistreatment) of all people of color classified as 'non-whites or non-Aryan' people by the people who classify them as 'white or Aryan'" (Cress Welsing 220)

Therefore, Cress Welsing (1991) demonstrates the existence of white supremacy in anti-Semitism, the bombing of Hiroshima and Nagasaki and Apartheid in South Africa. Besides Anti-Semitism, Slave trade and colonialism was part of Holocaust, a planned mass slaughter of the blacks. Responding to self-alienation also resulted

47

in mass murders in Congo and Namibia. The Herero people resistance of the German conquest, were put into concentration camps, driven to dry deserts as exile and killed by the Germans as to protect white supremacy. It is true to argue that, the challenge of white supremacy is psychological, it affects human behaviors to adopt the most lethal strategies to exist as a race in global sphere.

In 1994, almost nearly a million people belonging to Tutsi ethnic group were murdered by their fellow countryman resulted in the historical confrontations and hatred. If scholars treat Rwandan genocide as a result of historical confrontations, it becomes a challenge to find the solution, since it is a false problem, which is to say, in a more logical sense, a manifestation of problem. Mamndani (1998) logical analysis diagnosed the real problem of this genocide as an offspring of colonial legacy, since the hatred was colonially created by the colonialist to fed the strategy of divide and rule. Therefore, the post-colonial situation was influenced by colonial legacy. Colonialism is a process of political domination by foreign governments and the Berlin Conference of 1884-85 authorised the colonization of Africa. It illuminated in form of maintaining white supremacy. However, internal factors such as pre-colonial raids, poor governance and ethnic class based societies also played an equal role in the happening of the Rwandan genocide.

In the Middle East, millions were killed in the so called 'war on terror'. This justifiable holocaust is traceable to white supremacist, a response to self-alienation, thereby attempts to annihilate people of color through wars. Millions were killed in wars and by sanctions in Middles East, specifically Iran, Syria, Palestine, Iraq and Afghanistan which shows US military agenda to control the region

48

of Middle East politically and annihilate the Arabs as people of color who have the capacity to produce color and be capable of annihilating the white races. Arabs were accused of terrorism, hence the military inversions were justified.

Apart from this military or physical mass slaughter, the development of technology made it possible to kill people without physically being involved in the process of killing. It emerged as the most cruel, atrocious, veil, and extremely wicked in the history of humanity. Biological warfare methods, which was proved useful in First World War resulted in the outbreak of swine flu that killed millions in post-world war 1. HIV/AIDS also falls in line of the biological warfare conspiracies, scientist believed that it was originated from Africans contact with African Green Monkey (The Velvet Monkey). That's how media present it. Global information and media controlled by the west serves the interest of the white capitalist race since information is the most crucial aspect in human interaction, thereby the publication of African Green Monkey as the source of HIV/AIDS blinds the world of the main cause of the pandemic. The disease claim millions lives in Africa, simply explained the logic of the targets to the people of color (Arabs, Latinos and Blacks). The historical experience of the people of color contact with the white race is based on the construction of white supremacy as a response of fear, self-alienation and the feeling of genetic inadequacy. To prove the biological warfare nature of HIV and AIDS, British political scientist and geneticist states that,

"The question of whether new diseases could be used is of considerable interest, Velvet Monkey diseases (African

49

Green Monkey) may well be an example of a new cases of diseases causing organism. Handling of blood and tissue without precaution causes infections. It is unaffected by any antibiotic substances so far tried and is unrelated to any other organism. It causes fatality in some cases and can be infectious disease to man. It presumably is also Biological warfare interest. New diseases are continually appearing (Chikungunya and o'nyongo) fever for example. In addition to this, there are possibilities of virus and bacteria genetically manipulated to produce 'new-organism" (Nottingham and Cookson 1969:322)

In this regard, the logical framework of this perspective is aimed at proving the existence of Biological Warfare, but at this juncture who is the enemy? People of the color are the enemy of White race, not because there are aggressive but the genetic make-up of people of color threatens the genetic existence of white race leading to serious self-alienation and self-hate, therefore in compensatory discourse, the modern holocaust was launched. The Tuskegee experiment is the justifiable event. Ebola in West Africa claim thousands, the disease was allegedly men-made. Men-made, that is to say global society is patriarchal, and the western man responsible for these pandemics. What is it important in West Africa? West Africa post-colonial political systems characterised by military coups and ethnic civil wars. The region is a former colony of Britain, Portugal and France, therefore it experienced false start or flag independence, which is only political and the economic means of production were controlled by the West. This is what Kwame Nkrumah said, "neo-colonialism, the last stage of imperialism", therefore as white supremacist project marginalises other ethnic groups leading to the eruption of civil wars, those civil wars referred to as proxy wars, sponsored by the West (Chabal 2014). West Africa region is rich in mineral resources such as gold, oil, ivory and other precious minerals, that is the reason why the Ebola holocaust allegedly planted in West Africa and the rest of Africa, to exploit resources as to fed the livelihood of white supremacism.

The current global pandemic COVID-19 killed thousands of people around the world, mainly China, Europe and United States of America. It is believed that the diseases originated from bats in China, and Mr Donald Trump, the former US President, openly refer it as China-Virus. The conspiracy theory tabled the issue of China-US trade wars as the source of the pandemic, since US wanted to dominate the world economic and politics but the increasing potential of multipolar world from Far East Asia threatened the interests of Washington Foreign policy. Therefore, trade wars occurred. The Washington foreign policy in global politics is an extension of white supremacism (racism) or the method of implementing the psychological compensation of self-alienation against people of color. Chinese represents the yellow race, hence their dominance in global economics and politics act as the revolutionary movement against the white supremacist/patriarchal global structures of trade, economics, law and politics. Therefore, though it is not scientifically proven, it is alleged that the white race launch this biological warfare to wipe out the Chinese race as part of people of color. However, from other sources it is believed that it originated from the Chinese military conspiracy against the Western world. Therefore, it's more than trade wars but racial wars, which have effected on the people of color. The situation of COVID-19 management in American and European hospital is tense, since the most casualties are black people, segregated and receiving little attention. This a genocide, whereby at first the disease kill the white race, a myth published about the blacks as less contagious to the disease. Now blacks are the most victims and constitute a large percentage of the fatalities. However, this is just a conspiracy, obscure but the main point here is the concept of white supremacy in public spaces as the dominant normative order. On the other hand, some of these conspiracy theories provides an epistemic foundation of the dynamics of contemporary pandemics. However, they failed to give a true reality of the situation and acknowledging the border discussions of the causes of these pandemics. Another case of the conspiracy theories has been presented below.

> "If you attempt to understand biological and chemical warfare without understanding white supremacism, you will only be confused. If you attempt to understand the killing of gypsies in Germany, under the leadership of Adolph Hitler without understanding white supremacy you will only be confused. If you attempt to understand the holocaust of Semites of the Jewish religion in Europe from 1933-1945, wherein 6, 000, 000 Semites were slaughtered under conditions of mass deceit with the awareness of other western (white) powers, without understanding white supremacy (racism, anti-Semitism), you will only be bewildered and totally confused" (Cress Welsing 1991:294)

However, in acknowledging these points of departure as the reality of the Global affairs is quite controversial, since other factors such as climate change contributed imrnesely to the contemporary holocaust. This paper is not racist at all or themed at blaming white race, but the logical foundation of the arguments are based on objective orientation of political and psychological effects of racism to people of color and white race as well. In responding to the physchological fear of generic inadequacy, they resort to the most cruel and atrocious solutions to deal with the anatomic and psychological existence of people of color in global space. In studying the modern holocaust, Hitler's Anti-Semitism, AIDS Holocaust and COVID-19 pandemics, it is worth to connect it with white supremacism, since there are intimately related and these holocaust are a behavioral results of sustaining the white supremacism. The 21 century holocaust is not just about physical slaughter, but based on the use of chemical biological warfare and state apparatus to deal with the people of color. Of course the world is moving into a global village, cultural exchanges and the consciousness of internationalism or international nationalism led to peace, the white race numerical inadequacy and color deficient continue to be the source of confusions and upheavals. The thrust is to liberate the world from this malevolent behaviors castigated to the black community in the name of preserving white supremacy.

Chapter 5

After Rhodes Must Fall: Student Activism in Confronting the Cognitive Dissonance

Rhodes must fall was more than just a statue removal or uprising against the statue, it was a symbolic gesture to the demand of the end of racism and epistemic genocides in South African public universities. White supremacy is well known using symbols, visuals and objects as cognitive dissonance strategy, statutes played a most important imperialist and colonialist role, shaping the history of empire. It was a symbolic aspect of the relationship between the colonisers and colonised where hierarchical in nature, the colonisers imposed commands, laws, thoughts and behaviors to the colonised, in this case the colonised were subjects of colonial structures and cosmologies as well as objects of the imperial masters. What it means to decolonize the university? What is the meaning and relevance of university in Africa? This essay is aimed at giving an honest answer on these questions.

This relationship problematises the discourse of humanity, it was centered on the basis of the race. White race only defined as human beings, a proper reflection of human beings and enjoyed the citizenship of empire, however black people and all people of color were dehumanized, reduced to non-thinking objects and non-humans in the ghettos or reserves. For Maldonado-Torres (2016), in Fanonian meditations colonised subjects conscripted into residence called dames, a place of the "Wretched of the Earth/non-beings. The society is divided into zones, those of humans and non-humans gave birth to the most treacherous racial Manichean misanthropy, South Africa Apartheid regime was the good example of the system of sub-humanisation of the people of color, into caste system based on color line. Wynter (2014) adopts a Fanonian strategy or thinking of the defining a colonised being, paralyzed psychologically, demonised and socialized in the basis of tolerating white superiority as the natural schema of the society. It defined as diatopical hermeneutic. The system instrumentalised to consolidate colonialism, since it was difficult to colonise the cultural conscience of people.

Existentiality of black being in this condition, determined by the colonial experiences and colonial-colonised relations illuminates in the master-servant relationship. This non-humanness of black people did not end at the attainment of African Independence, it continued in the present era and we inherit this system from our fathers life in colonial times and it affects the way we think, the way we define ourselves and the way we relate with the outside world and the way we participate in epistemological development. We are always at the bottom page of scientific-epistemic inventions and reduced to objects which is defined as cognitive dissonance. Africans lost-self in the global space. Steve Biko was right, when he said "mind is the most potent weapons of the colonisers". This fund the project of white supremacy, the white race as they successfully managed to distort the original thinking of Africans, control the minds of the blacks through religious symbols and the western education. It reflects in African way of life emulating Europeans, use white being as epitome of beauty, white race as the source of economic salvation to Africans and self-hatred among black people's view of culture as expression of demonic and primitive system.

"The crucial issue here is that there was no intellectual means of distinguishing between European particularism and the universal functions it was supposed to incarnate, given that European universalism had constructed its identity precisely through the cancelation of the logic of incarnation and, as a result, through the universalization and so forth. The resistance of particular identities and cultures were as part of all embracing and epochal struggle between universality and particularisms-the nation of people without history expressing precisely their incapacity to represent the universal" (Laclau 1996:24)

Ernesto Laclau (1996) exposes the concepts of universalizing European particularisms as the methods of cognitive dominance. European thoughts and cultures as particular oriented and originated in Europe, universalised through colonialism and coloniality of political-cultural space. Christianity, western thoughts, modernity and western social phenomenon universalised. Anti-colonial used Eurocentric methods of liberation and after independence adopts western models of governances such as socialism and democracy as political blueprints in post-colonial state craft. Hence cognitive dissonance surface, consciously black realizes the existence of oppression through the lances of Eurocentric labels and concepts and adopts the methods as liberatory systems which continue to dismember Africaness. Nationalist led anti-colonial and decolonial movements were products of the western universities and the westernised universities in Africa as part of integrating them in European society, they launch the struggle against the system to achieve self-rule, but the colonial system continued in post-colonial era as manifestation of coloniality in colonised nationalists. Ndhlovu-Gatsheni (2018) argued that decoloniality was not part of the wider scale anti-colonial movements, embracing the same system which distorts the memory of black people.

Anti-colonial movements heralded by educated caliber, but alienated from the meaning of Africaness which distorts the applications of African freedom movements. They is need to scrutinizes the historic incidents led to the creation of those institutions providing African nationalist figures. Aristotlean logic and Catholic systems of thoughts claim monopoly of knowledge in medieval Europe. After great chain of being and enlightenment, western scholars criticised Catholic monopoly of economy of knowledge as a hindrance factor to innovation and development of independent thoughts. Rene Descartes led the critic, dethroning Catholics epistemic dominance and popularizes the template of thoughts based on existentialism of being and the relations with knowledge. It narrowly reduced the gap of the subject and object by giving credit to critical thinking to prove the existence of knowledge and defines the existence. "I think therefore I am", defines the western scholarship based on individuation of being ownership of knowledge. Rene Descartes philosophy dominates European cognizance in social science and physical science disciplines. Immanuel Kant philosophy of reasoning delimits the center of knowledge production located in Northern Europe, this determines the present systems of intellectual thoughts, whereby five countries U.S.A, Germany, France, Britain and Italy dominates arts, literature and theories of human relations.

Therefore, African leaders learn abroad, in the U.S, France and Britain who deposited the western patriarchal/capitalist/ racial epistemologies in their minds as authentic ways of thoughts, most of them used to brag for learning at the finest universities in the world but honestly they celebrates cognitive dissonance. Fanon (1967) states that, the most educated people are the most alienated and peasants must be the leading figures in decolonial movements as the victims of the colonial experiences, understands it better and able to give a true alternatives to colonial subjugations. Educated nationalists referred to as petty beougeosie, led policy formulations and continue to entrap Africans minds in the snare of western cognitive empire. "African history lie in the dark mantle and Africans are people without historical conscience", words from the Philosophy of History by Fredrich Nietzsche, this negative perspective of Africans dominates African studies for more than a century and it explained the curriculum or education systems revived by African nationalists abroad during colonial era, who were taught that their race has no history, therefore the history have and have-nots distinctions explains the mental abuse suffered by the Africans, an epistemic prison or intellectual detention. Amie Caesar, founded Negritude Humanism with Leopold Senghor at Sobourne University wrote "our fathers have no cathedral, no civilisations", explained how Europeans view Africa. Rhodes Must Fall sloganised decolonizing the curriculum which remained colonial through post-Apartheid education policies crafted by alienated policy makers, failed to recognize the mental confusion caused by colonialism. Around 1824, Fourah Bay College came into existence in Sierra Leone as affiliate college of University of Durham to train skilled laborers demanded in Western

Corporations and Civil Services and African universities such as University of Cape Town, Stellenbosch University, Ibadan University, Makererere University, and University of Zimbabwe to mention few formed as affiliate colleges of western universities. Curriculum was designed and controlled by the western universalizes, European particularisms and epistemology to alienate Africans from their roots, making them objects and fund the inferiority complex in social socialisation through education.

> "It is clear that another world cannot be possible as long as the continent and its people are not fully decolonized and the snares of the post-colonial neocolonised world are not broken. This will require an epistemic rebellion that enables the formerly colonised people to gain self-confidence, enabling them to re-imagine another world free from western tutelage" (Ndhlovu-Gatsheni 2013: 263-264)

To create a new world it is not possible to imagine it in Eurocentric complex or use Eurocentric methodology. Rhodes Must Fall presents an epistemic rebellion against the celebration of colonial history through the statue of the colonial icon Cecil John Rhodes, representing white supremacy, colonialism and coloniality of epistemology. Rhodes Must Fall immortalizes the ideas of Black Consciousness in South Africa, premised on explaining the African ghetto conditions resultant from mental dispossession, black inferiority, colonialism and apartheid. It centralises its discussion of minds as the potent weapons used by the oppressor to establish colonial rules. That is to say, colonialism, slavery and apartheid had psychological impacts of blacks, distorted the way we think and consume confidence and pride of the black people. This was sustained by cultural genocide, christianism and coloniality of epistemologies in education. Therefore, Black consciousness was a South African youth-student movement confronting apartheid, with vision to deconstruct the minds and unlearn cultural inferiority, black pride and create a nationalistic consciousness based on the mutual sufferings and the struggle for emancipation of the victims of apartheid. Strategically implemented through black projects, self-sustenance systems and the need to construct that mentality. It works hand in hand with Fanonian understanding of the discourses of colonialism, its mental effects and the decolonial alternatives, whereby he argued that, peasants need to decolonize the mind through unlearning western patterns of thoughts and violent rebellion (Maldonado-Torres 2018).

Black Consciousness creates Azania People's Organization (AZAPO) and South Africa Student Organization (SASO) as the revolutionary structures to continue the anti-apartheid launched by imprisoned Nelson Mandela and Robert Mangaliso Sobukwe. South Africa student revolted against the relegation of African languages, which was the first epistemic freedom movements in the history of education in Africa, however the event unfolds in bloodshed, demonstrators gunned down in the streets of Soweto by Police, defending Apartheid regimes and white supremacy. In 1977, Steve Biko was assassinated in Police custody. Steve Biko Legacy "I will write what I want", confronts apartheid and the grave Soweto massacre still act as the source of modern South African Student Activism. The movements aimed at defining the meaning of the university to Africans not as place of alienation but of learning Africaness and Afrocentric thoughts in physical science and social science as well as to end racism in public universities.

In post-apartheid South Africa, academic was blackened as anti-racist motives but they failed to blacken epistemologies and white supremacy continue in thought systems to fund the cognitive dominance and cognitive dissonance against the black people. Therefore, an angry students at the University of Cape Town in 2015 demands the removal of Rhodes statue and decolonisation of education, the movement was also intercontinental, at Oxford University Rhodes Must Fall activism also demands the removal of Rhodes statue as symbol of white supremacy and the traumatic history of colonialism. This activism promotes intellectual creativity and imagination which led to the publication of the collection of essays, poetry and stories in the book *Rhodes Must Fall: The struggle to decolonize heart of racist empire*. Fees Must Fall demands the founding of black students to 'massify' education as decolonial strategy actively decampanings racist injustices at the university. Therefore, social activism is a necessary step to challenge the epistemic oppression of black people, subjectivism and objectivism as theorising art and erotic and the struggle to unlearn the westernised thoughts channeled by the victims, the academic peasants (Maldonado-Torres 2016).

Therefore, the movement defines decolonisation of education as a process, a system and end product of generating colonially dismembered African thoughts in learning humanities and social sciences at the universities and public schools to promote black pride, annihilates inferiority complex and racism at campuses. In this regard, to decolonize the university is not just to Africanise but remember the dismembered and establish a pluriversal template of thoughts which is multicultural and multi-centric, hence dismantle the Eurocentric monopoly of world view.

After Rhodes Must Fall, a decolonial consciousness spread across the country, the continent and universalised from the Latin scholars, the topic presented in colloquiums, conferences, symposiums and seminars, debated, refined and educational policies designed in decolonial paradigm. Gandhi Must Fall was also another student revolt at University of Ghana, demanding the removal of Gandhi statue at campus, accused of being a racist, representing upper-caste Hindus or Indo-Aryans and relegating black people in Africa and South India. Mahatma Gandhi referred Africans as 'heathens', 'barbarians' and 'animals' though apologist of Gandhi publicise the image of a great non-violent leader and the peace maker. The revolution led by Professor Obadele Kombon, a research fellow and a professor of African Studies in Institute of African Studies at the University of Ghana. The increase of these student revolts played a most important role in epistemic struggle and epistemic liberties from mental slavery. Decolonising the university is the pre-requisite of global peace, student movements or students as the victims must continue to embrace epistemic rebellion to dismantle the western dominated empire.

Chapter 6

Women of Color in men-made 21st Century: The praxis of Global South feminisms

For Thomas Sankara "social liberation without woman liberation is meaningless". That is to say, social liberation was not a sexist driven liberation but encompasses everyone victimised by systematic racism and colonialism. Anti-colonial movements was not just aimed to decolonize political space but an antidote to white supremacy as a system propagates cognitive dissonance to the people of color. Thereby it is meaningless to claim we are liberated when the other group are still oppressed by virtues of being a woman, at same time people of color, decolonisation was a wholesale movements to deconstruct the Eurocentric/patriarchal/capitalist cosmology. This essay attempts to give a critical reflections of thoughts of the positions of woman in global social space in the 21st century founded on the first generation of woman activisms.

The world today is men-made, patriarchal constructed. The 21st century is celebrated as the age of post-humanistic civilisation, however, it reflects men-made, it is a brainchild from the patriarchal society, therefore the plight of woman, black woman in particular need to be considered. The world is man-made as it is today, those scientific and technological advancement the world celebrates are the inventions of patriarchal epistemology, Einstein relativity theory and other physical scientist dominates the disciplines. White woman though subjugated, they increased proximity to the access and contributes to scientific and scholastic development but like the man of color, woman of color still relegated to the periphery and the road is still far for woman to participate in knowledge making. The world arrive to that point after the fall of Grenada in 1492, Indian woman/woman of color in Iberian Peninsula were philosophers, burnt alive, accused of witchcraft due to their cosmic philosophical understanding. The response by white male based on Catholic tradition counter threat from woman of color in knowledge (Grosfoguel 2013). This is justified by the non-existence of woman in the development of social theory and physical science knowledge in the contemporary discourses.

Therefore, 21st century boast of human civilisation, but the civility of human beings distorted by the existence of racism and sexism as social normative order. From Iberian Peninsula, the so called "Dark Continent", "barbarism", "people without soul" and "people without history" as from Eurocentric perspectives, glimpses and light of cosmos knowledge demystified by the imperialist through slavery and imperialism. In antiquity, African societies were based on gender balance as the dominant social cosmology. The concept of "I am because we are" is the foundational basis of African epistemology, cosmology, ontology and ethics (Wiredu 2002), the formation this social philosophies was not patriarchal centered neither discriminatory, but it was inclusive, includes man and woman, children and outcast. The society was integrative, so as social outcomes such as perceptions, social values and the systems of thoughts. What went wrong? Colonialism exports Catholic/patriarchal values to Africa, woman disposed from their natural rights, reduced to the domestic chores and their economic social values was distorted, whereby in need of labor white farms and industries hire man, train them. That is why man become

64

powerful, start to own means of production, properties and wealth and access to education. This creates a hierarchical social structure, dismembered social equality since time immemorial in African set up.

Colonialism was at the same time dispossession, theft, plunder, killing, alienation, distortions, demonization, sub-humanisation and dehumanization of African Being, violently disposed from the existing cultural legacy funds the spiritual consciousness of black being. Therefore, the applications of Eurocentric gender and feminism concepts in African society is a death theory, resulted in numerous divorces, male-female violences and hostilities since it failed to define the real problem, roles and position of man and woman in the African settings. 21st Century feminism is man-made, though invented by Woman following the legacy of Suffragettes, Mary Wollstonecraft and Mary Astell, but the foundational thoughts were sexist epistemology that failed to go beyond patriarchal systems of thoughts, used patriarchal paradigms to dismantle it that led to chronic social paranoia and crisis. Feminism as anti-thesis to chauvinism, it is a source of confusion in African set-up, whereby it has nothing African in the emancipatory movement, it is designed for the white people. If it means to materialize, woman subjectivism will not end, oppression of black woman by white woman, racial inequality and social inequality will always be a factor that affects the materialization of this movement.

Fortunately, Post-modern feminism seeks to solve the challenge of racial inequalities, premised on the realisation of reason and global inequalities, premised on the realisation of racism and global inequalities as competing to the patriarchal structures in marginalizing woman of color. The setting of the world is embeds on racism/white supremacy, therefore people of color (man and woman) are subjects to that system that corroborates the hierarchical orientations of the global order, based on dichotomy of white supremacy and black inferiority. Woman of color as part of Black Nation, described in the categories if racial derogatory terms, heathen, dirty, sub-humans and non-humans. This is a problem of the 21st century, people claim civilisation and non-existence derogatory racial insults, but it happens every day, consciously or unconsciously in the complex systems of global modernity built of the foundation of racism. Butler (2010), Dangarembga (2002), Vera (2000) proposes a deconstruction frameworks based on woman economic empowerment, inclusions in developmental space and dismantle racism. This method bring woman of color near to liberation, but remains in the chains of mental slavery since it embrace the system that dispossess them as alternative to the 'burden of womanhood' (Dangarembga 2002, Chimamanda Adichie 2012). The man-made or patriarchal controlled epistemology used as foundation disciplines of the question of woman results in the contemporary perpetuity of woman oppression.

Africana Womanism, together with Afrocentric feminism defines woman being using African agency and proposes an alternative to colonially constructed oppressive systems such as racism, sexism and self-alienation aspects. Instead of emancipatory woman in 21st century, racism and sexism continue to alienate woman of color from their African family hood (Mazama 2003). Therefore, Mazama (2003) argued that, Afrocentric consciousness is a liberatory system to remember the dismembered African social systems, settings and world views. The theory talk about beauty of Africans, melanin and Afro-natural hair movement of Africana womanism, install pride and confidence to the woman of color to define beauty in their own set up. Afrocentric theory proposed woman liberation based on remembered cultural values dismembered by violent colonialism which vandalizes the sense of family hood in the African set up. 'Boarder Thinking' and decolonial feminism exposes the patriarchal nature, seeks to promote woman involvement in academic space and knowledge production, mainly woman of color participates in the decoloniality of epistemology (Lugones 2013 and Anzaldua 1983). "Boarder thinking" is anti-thesis of the coloniality of the logics, based on the realisation of oppression mentally and develop and delink from the system (Anzaldua 1983). Therefore, to promote woman of color liberation boarder thinking, Afrocentric feminism and Africana womanism provides a tangible solutions to race and gender problem.

Epidemics (HIV/AIDS, Ebola and COVID-19), wars (war on terror, ethnic induced conflicts), economic conundrum problematises the whole scale existence of woman of color in global space. These crisis are man-made but affects mostly woman, woman are the major victims psychologically and sociologically, left with orphans, divorced and suffer from woman related issues. Another challenge is, 21st century claimed to be civilized, taught woman to be empowered, but failed to teach man how to live with an empowered woman, this is need for a cultural rethink, mental shift need adaption and adaptation can be taught as well. This remain a serious milestone to the achievement of a meaningful democratic space in the contemporary world, instead of liberating woman, it distance them, alienates them from the society. Woman issue is not mono-sex centered struggle but a human struggle, therefore integration is the possible solution to materialize woman rights in the man-made 21st century.

Chapter 7

Islamophobia and Islamic Freedom Fighters: Anti-Racism perspective in Islamism.

The war against people of color is now given another name, 'war on terror'. Though it was a response against the 9/11 attacks by the Islamist militants, but to my opinion it is worth to qualify it as war on people of color, whereby the concept of terrorism is synonymously used to refer to the Muslims and Arab nationalism and liberation freedom. It is Eurocentric in nature, since they is need to carefully scrutinize the reason behind these militants movements, it's not deliberate or enjoys the mass killing of people through suicide bombs but premised on genuine reasons and it is founded that, these genuine reasons are focused on anti-imperialism, social injustices and fighting than despotic politicians. Why I call it a war of people of color, like the Jews, Arabs belong to the Semites group, mixed breed with blacks and hence they have capacity to produce color which threatens the white race existentiality in the global space. Therefore, the frustration resulted from self-alienation and fear of numerical inadequacy drive white race to impose control to the Arabs and sent the symbolic gesture of white superiority and the inferiority of the Arabs. The involvement of United States and White Race in Arabian Peninsula led to the Arabian Holocaust, which in this essay I also claim the slogan, "Arabs Lives Matter".

The war against Semites is too ancient than it is presented starting from Hitler Anti-Semitism. The fall of Grenada in 1497 led to serious persecution of people of Arab and African Origins in Iberian Peninsula, referred to Marranos and Morriscos, this were

69

Christian converts, converted from Muslims and Judaism. This Judeophobic and Islamophobic concept, have its roots in the early Christian crusaders defeated by the Muslim Sultans and driven away from the so-called Holy Land, Jerusalem. Therefore, the hatred between Europeans and Arabs were basically religious issue, however beyond the religious empathy, the color prejudices also surface, since Jews and Muslims belong to the people of color, Yellow race and white race fear genetic competition from these races, therefore Racism extend also to Arab and Hebrews (Semites) as non-whites.

After 9/11 attack, a new form of racism emerge propagated by the western media and better explained in post-structural perspective of the contact between European self and the other (Islamic world). Islamophobia (Love 2017 and Kumar 2012) rise as the new anti-Semitism racist behavior towards the Muslims and Islamic being across the world. It is referred to as new Anti-Semitism of Anti-Semitism of 21st century, a racist behavior against people of color. According to Jenkins (2016), it is a social reality that shapes arguments in social science and law about the extension of racism or the birth of neo-racism (Balibar 1991).

The term problematically defined and raised debates whereby scholars failed to identify the aspects that constitutes Islamophobia it is not based on conceptual analysis but sustained by examples (Bleich 2012). According to Bleich (2012) Islamophobia is premised on racism and it is a form of racism that targets the expression of "Muslimness" sustained in media, political speeches and books. However the idea is entrenched in examples than phenomenal context that raises debates. For Mehdi (2010),

70

Islamophobia developed in the late 1990s as a political concept aimed at explaining the causes, dynamics, course and consequences of anti-Islam, to comprehend Islamophobia, the history of Islam is much needed whereby Christian crusaders stimulates the construction of racial hatred towards Islamic faith, hence the implementation of it in anti-Islamic refugee's laws by Donald Trump referred to as neo-Christian crusades.

Said (2003) structural analysis of racism creates a comprehensive thought in understanding the genealogy of Islamophobia. Firstly the creation of Occident (European self-West) and Orient (The other-East of Europe) on the basis of European supremacist sustained by Friedrich Hegel Philosophy of History in hierarchizing the society, Secondly, the treatment of the other as non-being, an inferior being from the Occident-Christian rational beings (Lezra 2010), thirdly is the power construction between the occident and the west, based on intersubjectivity and colonialism (Butler 1990). In doing so, Balibar (1991) develops the concept of Arabophobia (the confusion of Arabness and Islamism), later on help to develop the concept of Islamophobia. From Said (2003) and Lomba (2003) theoretical proposition, the dehumanization of the East worsened by 9/11 attack, insults and hatred speeches, whereby Islam referred to as barbaric, non-humans, war mongers, fascist and oppressive from the western media. These attacks are referred to as Islamophobia. All Part Group in British Parliament, defines Islamophobia as follows

> "Making mendacious, dehumanizing, demonizing, or stereotypical allegations about Muslims as such, or of Muslims as a collective group. Such as, especially but not exclusively, conspiracies about

Muslim entrism in political government or other societal institutions. The myth of Muslim identity having a unique propensity for terrorism, and claims of demographic 'threat' posed by Muslims or of a Muslim takeover"

In this regard, the attack of Muslims due to the expression of Muslimness constitute Islamophobia, however the term raises a lot of debate and controversies, remain in the periphery of social science analysis and denied entry in legal system as protective mechanism to the Muslims (Vakil 2009). There is a difference between anti-Islamism and anti-Muslims, whereby the former is about the hatred of the religion and the latter is about the hatred of Islamic being, but it all constitute Islamophobia. As neo-racist perspective, the Islamic resistance on confronting the western world suffers persecution, bad images and hatred around the golem hence this term constitute a broader spectrum in developing an empirical knowledge about Islamic resistance and confronting the western world.

Why Islam? Nation of Islam as founded by the Afro-Americans to confront the unjust world and use Islamism as an ideology of liberation exacerbated by the racial hatred and the feeling of self-alienation by the white race. Afro-Americans in Haiti and the Caribbean's use Yoruba spirituality for the liberation of the soul and maintain Black identity, but Nation of Islam (NOI) use Islam religion to strengthen the anti-racism spiritual movements, deviates from the Whitened Christianity historically that marginalises the Black race. The problem which Christianity is, it taught slaves to obey to their slave-masters, abandon their cultural existence and also facilitates colonialism. The famous Valladolid Judgment also

72

was conducted by the Christians, and act as the historic event in justifying the enslavement of Africans, referred to as people without soul.

The symbolic paintings of White Jesus and White God in Cathedral and Chapels serves the interest of white race, psychologically denigrates the confidence of people of color's existence as human beings and their closeness to the spiritual being. The image of God colonised, at the same time with the image of black people also colonised and distorted. For Cress Welsing (1991), white supremacy is sustained by the use of symbols because of its spiritual and psychological impacts to the spiritually conscious people of color. In response the racist perspective of Christianity and the Image of God, Islam postulates that, clay was used to create first human being, therefore there is no white clay from soil science perspective, there is red or black clay soil, meaning to say if God use clay soil to create first human being in his own image, the race of God must be black or red and the first human being to be created must be black or red. This is just a hypothesis, but my point here is, outside African religions, Islam appears to be non-racist as compared to Christianity, though values and teachings are the same.

Therefore, Islam was the hope of Afro-Americans, and Nation of Islam attracts large audience from the poor black communities. Besides its link to the Afro-American, it originated in Mecca, from the Qurayish Tribe founded by Ishmael, son of Abraham. The features of the race were yellow people, described as dark race in the history of the Bible, therefore these people have ability to produce color as their genetic inheritance, and therefore the fear of genetic annihilation among white race resulted to the existence of logic, speeches, behaviors and actions against the religion itself. Nation of Islam claim itself as the Lost Tribe of Shabazz, under the leadership of Elijah Muhammad and Minister Louis Farrakhan and recognized as part of the global scale Muslim movement. Malcom X was the member of Nation of Islam (NOI), criticised openly racism, mental slavery and civil disobedience and violent strategy opposed to Martin Luther King Junior non-violence movement against white supremacism. Nation of Islam under the influence of Malcom X consciously led to the realisation of mental slavery, hence intellectual independence was the strategy to fight the continuous ignorance and victimization of Black people, hence through Islam education intellectual independence among black community, to start thinking not as the other but as black person was to be achieved through delinking from the mainstream westernised education and adopts black and Islamic education.

In most cases, Malcom X and Martin Luther were portrayed as enemies by the western-centric perspectives, but there were not enemies, belonged to same race, have the mutual understanding of the inferiorization of the blacks, but they differ in the strategies to fight racism and all strategies were worthy, spirited by the same objective to liberate people of color or African descent from mental slavery and brutal political injustices in the USA and beyond. Prophet Muhammad (Peace Be upon Him) and Jesus Christ belong to the Semites races. The painting in Madonna portrays Mary the Mother of Jesus as Black (Clarke 1998). Therefore, hatred against the Muslim religion is about its non-racial teachings and used as a source of hope during the time of civil rights Movements. In contemporary cosmogony, the Muslims people fight against racism presented in form of Islamophobia, but their fights are regarded as terrorism, a crime against humanity and the leader of those extremist movements are eliminated. Though these extremist movements go beyond the Islamic ethics of war, which prohibits the killing of innocent people, destruction of property but they wage war to the aggressors only. It is founded that, the use of suicide bombings is heretic to Islam whereby innocent people killed are opposed to fundamental principle of Jihad, but is embedded on genuine reasons to launch the struggle, beyond Islamic teachings to confront the existing westernised universe.

Western civilisation in this case is beyond geopolitical location, but defines the complexity of white supremacism built in psychological self-alienation and fearing genetic color competition, influencing the systematic existentiality of racism in law, politics, education and all facets of life. Western civilisation is based on capitalism, as economic and social model strengthened individualism and white supremacy, since people of color across the world believe in cosmopolitan discourse of the society resulted in the existence of African nationalism, Confucianism, Satyagraha and other social-cultural models. These non-western social philosophy are more lucrative, subliminal and attractable, therefore the involvement of materialism in white supremacy aimed to out-mode those theories. Western civilisation is now beyond western boarders but forced to non-white races through media, politics and education.

> "The western ways of thought… (Have) an enmity towards all religions, and in particular with greater hostility towards Islam. The enmity towards Islam is especially pronounced and many times is the result of a

well thought-out scheme the object of which to demolish the structure of Muslim society" (Qutb 1964:11)

The enmity towards other cultural issues is about them as source of pride to people of color and the ability to influence the color consciousness, self-liberation and pride which threatens the existence of white supremacy. Ubuntu gloriously prescribed on cultural-social belonging of oneself and it was once demonised, Islamic religion provides the prescription of social justice and equality among all races and remain an enemy to the West. Qutb **Sayyid** concurs that, the West hates all religions, Islam, African Spiritual Cosmology, Taoism, Buddhism, Hinduism, Confucianism and other various religions around the world, because all these religions poses threats to the existential of western sponsored global injustices. Qutb **Sayed argued that,** the greater hostility is towards Islam, since it resist thousands of years and today, it outweighs the westernised Christianity and shows the possibility of dominating the world. Therefore, it is synonymously referred to as terrorism, extremism. From the Post-structural perspective, meta-narratives constructed by the western established scholarship ignore genuine grievances on Islamic militants and term them terrorist.

> "In more than 60% of cases, the words 'violent', 'death', 'attack', 'kill', 'suicide' or 'gunmen' were in close proximity to the words 'Arabs', 'Palestinians', 'Muslim' or 'Islam' (Manning 2010)

In this regard, the western centered-narratives denigrates the Image of Muslims and Islam. The so called terrorist organisations are

76

fighting the western cognitive empire and its forms of knowledge premised on Cartesian forms of thoughts. The religion is a threat to white supremacy compensatory system.

"Western education is Christian-cum-atheist in orientation. It seeks to dismantle Islamic religious narratives and their political social implications. On a political perspective, I think religion as fundamental belief system, and fundamental knowledge base plays a pivotal role in shaping ideology, philosophy and norms within a particular societies, as such dismantling of Islamic religious people and believers transcend to epistemicide of all Islamic societies. That lead to epistemological vulnerabilities, destruction of moral ethics and norms, and more disgustingly and regrettably, epistemological hegemony of the west and its politico-economic implications. On social level, western education insults Islamic identity by being amoral and apathetic. It also veralises Christian values, which seem too exclusive in their definition of morality, justices and right that leads to deviant behavior amongst religious societies and that is something the Muslim world, particularly" (Interview with Brendon Kasirisiri)

In a conversation of with Brendon Kasirisiri, the above was his thoughts on the existence of westernised cognitive empire towards Islam. Therefore, it explains the construction of Islamism ideology, as political philosophy adopts Islamic principle in liberating people and global space from the complex white supremacy, which affects not only politics but as well the mind, the way we think and see things in the global perspectives. This behavior of epistemicide, influenced by the psychological fear of genetic and epistemic annihilation of the white race due to their numeric disadvantage and color genetic incapacity. Boko Haram, Al-Shabab, Al-Qaeda to mention a few resists the western world.

Chapter 8

Anti-colonial Legacy of Bob Marley: Decolonial Singing in Reggae Music

Afro-Carribean reggae music spreads bullets of resistance to white supremacy, re-awakening the revolutionary consciousness, spiritual movements and confidence to fight the Babylon system. Jamaican dancehall, reggae and Afro-Jazz music popularly known for liberation songs. They transform emotions into words, sing to the world about the suffering, injustices, and inequalities and steer revolutionary consciousness among the victims. The thrust of this essay is to critically examine the decolonial credence in the iconic Bob Marley reggae music themed at exposing the Babylon system (white supremacy), sing the experiences of the Afro-American and Africans under slavery and colonial system, the mental confusion co-authored by western supremacy and proposed a decolonial framework to the problem. Bob Marley was the voice of Afro-Caribbean, Afro-Americans and Africans, he was a prophet, a liberation fighter, fighting through music, a dedicated cadre to peace and love, his music stole the hearts of millions referred to as the decolonial frameworks and it is still relevant in the contemporary. The reflections of reggae music in modern world is premised on Rastafarianism, African identity, anti-racism and composes ghetto social experiences into musical words.

Bob Marley as the icon of anti-white supremacy in reggae music, was born on 6 February 1945 at the farm in Nine Mile, Saint An Parish, Jamaica to the British Naval Officers Sinclair Marley and

Afro-Jamaican Cadella Malcom. He identified himself as African, despites being of interracial parents as a result of rural livelihoods. Bob Marley full name is Robert Nesta Marley. At the age of 12, he moved to Trenchtown in Kingston, a ghetto town. Afro-Jamaican are relegated to the ghetto but provides a fertile ground for revolutionary consciousness, adopts Pan Africanist-Marxist view of social liberation in the ghettos of Jamaica. The legacy of Marcus Garvey, C.L.R. James, Amy Jacques-Garvey, Fidel Castro and Che-Guevara were inspiration to new generation of activists, artists and intellectuals in the 1960s Afro-Caribbean nationalistic consciousness. These notable figures influenced by "Harlem Renaissance and Haiti Revolution" as the historical legacy in Caribbean political theatre, the realisation of oppression, history of slave trade, social injustices, colonialism and racism instilled critical thinking to the new generations. Therefore, in this situation Bob Marley become the voice, together with Peter Tosh, Bunny Wailer, Junior Braithwaite and Beverley Kesclo under the group called Wailing Rudeboys, changed later to wailing wailers in 1963. In this regard, to comprehend the message of Bob Marley, his background is important, he grew up in rural areas and ghetto, in poverty stricken society were social injustices based on color prejudices act as the cornerstone of the sociological schema and policies.

> "Marley wasn't singing about how peace could come easily to the world but rather how he on Earth comes too to many. His songs were his memories, he had lived with the wretched, he had seen the down pressers and those whom they pressed down" (Gilmore 2013:61)

His lyrical content, were highly political, themed on liberation of the African people in diaspora and in Africa, influenced by the metaphysical environment of the complex white supremacy and racism, which he referred to as Babylon. Bob Marley compose numerous albums, a mixture of reggae, rock and roll and ska won numerous awards such as Peace Medal of third World countries in 1978 by the United Nations humored by Jamaican government and his song "one love" named a song of the century by BBC. Today, he still lives, inspires people to promote peace, love and anti-racism.

Bob Marley Discography include The Wailing Wailers (1965), Soul Rebels (1970), Soul Revolution (1971) Catch a Fire (1973), Burnin (1973), Natty Dread (1974), Kaya (1978), Survival (1979), Uprising (1980) and Confrontation (1983). Bob Marley Anti-colonial struggle and Pan African legacy stemmed on his conversion from Catholic to Rastafarianism in 1965, Catholic was more oppressive that time, justified slavery and colonialism, in Valladolid judgment (1550-51) and the role of Catholic priests in colonialism, however Rastafarianism developed as religion that prescribes the situation of black people and related them to the chosen race or Solomonic dynasty, where Africa is the actual Zion, Marijuana as sacrament and Emperor Haile Selassie a son of God. The presentations of the black people in Rastafarianism attracts millions of black people around the world to join the religion as the divine revolutionary spiritual movement against Babylon. Babylon refereed to modern civilisation as an offshoot of slavery, colonialism and neo-colonialism characterised by immoral sociological schema of social injustices, exploitations and racism (Abayomi 2002). This metaphysical cultures responsible for creating inferior beings reflected in Afro-Caribbean, Afro-Americans and Africans, treated as non-beings and subjects of white supremacy, Muslims referred

81

the West as Infidels as a result of systematic racism and its massacre project in the name of war on terror in the Middle East, Rastafarians also referred them as Babylon empire as a result of the racial and shocking practice of social injustices in contemporary westernised world.

"Babylon system is the vampire, yea (vampire)
Sucking the children day by day, me say the Babylon system is Vampire,
Falling empire sucking the blood of the suffers, yeah
Building church and university, deceiving the people continually
Me I say them graduation thieves and murders.
Look out now they sucking the blood of sufferers."

These thoughts, descriptions of the existentiality of Babylon; Gregory Isaac also sung about Babylon, a westernised empire built on the foundation of racism systems and sub-humanising people of color. The system is vampire, a vampire survivors on the blood of suffers, and their fortunes build on the sweat, suffering, blood and tears of people of color, black people in particular. Today, the western world boast of its development, subliminal infrastructures, wealth and civilized social values, but no one can forget slavery, black people shipped from Africa to America to work in plantations so as to build Washington, resources transported from Africa accessed through exploitation to build magnificent Brussels, London, Amsterdam and Paris. Europeans enjoyed civilisation whilst Africans are in grief, there is no development or under-development of the global south which is linked to the ruthless dispossession, geopolitical structures colonially constructed of the core and periphery as well as part of imperial colonialism as part of Imperial projects. This situation manifest in modern world, the capitalist global cosmogony embrace neo-colonialism in exploiting the resources of South at a cheaper price and still at an exorbitant prices to the global south. Mazrui (1983) states that, the problem with Africa is it consumes what it does not produce and produce what it does not consume. It's not African fault, but global set up of the economic zones. Babylon is Vampire, Babylon is too rough.

> "Building churches and universities', these institutions were there to serve white supremacy through brainwashing African minds to think as inferior beings, unfortunate race and destined to subjugations. Churches and universities were a symbol of oppression to vandalize the truth about Africans and participates in epistemic and cultural genocide".

The history is falsified, colonization justified in church, brainwash through painting the color of God and angels as whites which alienates people of color from the spiritual consciousness. Cater G Woodson (1953) states that, the miseducation of the Negro continues to alienates, enslave and dehumanizes people of color in academic and social space. And this miseducation funded by the justification of slavery as mission civilistrice. This is what Bob Marley calls *emancipate ourselves from mental slavery* in Redemption song, *rebel and tell the children about slavery and the glory of Africa in Babylon songs.*

These conditions influences Marcus Garvey, W.E.B. DuBois, George Padmore, Stomikael Garmichael to form Pan Africanism on the grounds of Marxism and the experiences, Afro-Caribbean and Afro-Americans to trace the roots, liberate the soul of Black people and back to Africa which was successfully implemented Liberian state project. Babylon is a vampire state sucking the blood of sufferers. For Isaac Gregory it is too rough and Peter Tosh as one of the pioneers of reggae defines a Vampire state as world of exploitation sexploitation of poor by rich, drained blood by the capitalist. In the song equal rights, Peter Tosh criticised openly the superior-inferior racial social schema as the source of evil and need to be deconstructed to create the genuine existence of peace in the global world.

Bob Marley criticised South African Apartheid and systematic races, linked to the project of dehumanization, dismembering of African forms of pride, confidence and treated as third class citizens or subjects.

"Until the philosophy which had one race superior and other inferior is finally, and permanently discredited.
And Abandoned everywhere is war. Me say war.
That until there is no longer first class citizens and second class of citizens of any nation.
Until the color of man's skin is of no more significant than the color of his eyes".

Therefore, this shows a clear dedication of reggae icon Bob Marley to world peace, since world cannot enjoy peace if racism is there as social phenomenon. Racism responded to self-alienation and self-hate of the white people, fearing genetic competition with people of color, therefore segregation in education, law, politics, religion initiated to create white superiority and black inferiority as compensatory system to the white race from psychological self-alienation. The policy of Apartheid in South Africa was stemmed on social hierarchy, whites as first class citizens enjoyed privileges, whilst blacks as third class citizens dehumanized and sub-humanised by the Apartheid policy of separate development, were conscripted in ghettos and were restricted movements to white residence, clubs and bars. Manganyi (1974) explained the existentiality of black being in a whitened world or being black in the world based on the experiences of degradations of black beings through racial treatments premised on the myth of the originality, civility and superiority of white race as justifying factor to colonialism. Today, they is still war, though the system is no longer there as legal system in post-1994 South Africa but it exists in a way of thinking influences behaviors, logics, speeches among black Africans, as people without confidence and pride, a lost generation, convinced to believe that black people are ugly, black skin is a badge of shame hence burn themselves with chemical-cosmetic to be whiter like snow to qualify in the circle of white race yet cultivating skin cancer and psychological alienation to African identity. Racism is the capitalistic order, a neoliberal order of states arrangements through Eurocentric development templates and also in the police institutions exemplified by the brutal murder of Gorge Floyd.

Pacifist scholars declared the world of peace after First World War, but the happening of Cold War and Islamist insurgency challenged the claim, today racism claimed millions of people, it continued to kill people of color systematically through sanctions, trade sabotage, biological weapons and anthropogenic climate induced disasters, hence we are still at war. "The dream of lasting peace, world citizenship, rule of international morality will remain but a flirting illusion to be pursued". Bob Marley supports Africa liberation in the Song "Zimbabwe" (1979), justified armed struggle as antidote to the Babylon holocaust. Most of the Liberation struggles in Southern Africa implemented militarily in Mozambique, Angola, Namibia and Zimbabwe. Frantz Fanon, Amilcar Cabral and Samora Machel and other military nationalist leader support and adopts guerrilla warfare as method of liberation, unchained Africans from brutal despotic colonial governments and successfully defeats anti-revolutionary forces. In the song war, he advocates for decolonisation in South Africa, Angola and Mozambique and engages in the prophetic thoughts of war in the East, war in the South, war in the North and war in the west, 'black lives matter, Islamic insurgency, Chinese thwarting US military project, the rise of decoloniality through student revolts in South Africa and anti-imperialist struggles in Cuba and Venezuela fulfil the words of Bob Marley, as long as racism is still there the world would not know peace. He was ahead of his time and Rastafarian seer together with Peter Tosh, Bunny Wailers, Buju Bunton and other notable Rastafarian reggae musicians, speaking about racial equality "we Africans will fight, we find it necessary and we know we shall win as we are confident" (Bob Marley). We shall fight as united continent, as united black people across the world, fight racism, fight imperialism and fight neo-colonialism.

Pan Africanism as social-cultural and intellectual movements to rebut the African inferiority, Kwame Nkurumah, Julius Nyerere, Patrice Emery Lumumba, and Emperor Haile Selassie find it necessary for Africans to unite and fight effectively against imperialism (Mahomva 2014). Bob Marley joins unity activists, believe in unity as a means to successfully outdo colonialism, neo-colonialism and systematic racism. In Bob Marley's perspectives, this unity is in two-fold as it is presented by the lyrics of the song

"Africa Unite" composed after the speech of his Imperial Majesty, Haile Selassie 1

"Africa unite. Cause we're moving right out of Babylon
And we're going to our fathers land. How good and how pleasant it would be
Before God and Man.
To see the unification of all African, yeah it's been said already…
Africa Unite!
Unite for the benefit of your people!
Unite for its later (Africa Unite) than you think!
Unite for its later (Africa uniting) than you think!
Africa awaits (Africa unite) its creators.
Africa awaiting (Africa uniting) its creators!
Africa you 'are my (Africa unite) forefathers cornerstone.
Unite for the Africans abroad
Unite for the Africa (unite) a yard."

This song, expressed Bob Marley's Pan African commitment to African unity with Africans abroad since the struggle of racism in Afro-Caribbean and Afro-Americans on African problems, her sons and daughters abroad suffer in the knees of racism and the challenge of colonialism and neo-colonialism is not only for Africans in Africa but also in diaspora since Africa is a big family, united by the origins, cultures and the history of dispossession. Marcus Garvey Universal Negro Improvement envision back to Africa dream, the return of Buffalo soldier to Africa reunite with their brothers and kinsman, survives the fierce fire in the furnace of Babylon, Return to Zion. W.E.B DuBois, Stomikael Garmichael an Afro-Trinidadian and thousands Afro-American return to Africa in post-independence to connect themselves with their roots, since people without culture are like tree without roots. Africa is the Zion of all Africans. Most celebrated Hollywood such as Michael Jai White traces their roots in Africa, end in Ghana and the 'project of back to Africa' did not end in the creation of Liberia, it is still relevant today, Afro-Americans are coming home, out of Babylon.

Bob Marley realizes importance of unity to Africa, what it means to African people, organization of African Union (OAU) under the philosophy of continental consciencism, Uhuru naumoja and Pan Africanism for self-reliance and African personality. This unity promotes independence, whereby in 1957 Kwame Nkrumah unselfishly stated that, "the independence of Ghana is meaningless if it is not linked to the total liberation of Africa", dedicated Ghana's resources to materialize the dream of African unity and help African states to achieve independence. "Africa awaits its creators", because it was Europe invention, nationalist founding fathers spearhead the process of Africa's re-membering and re-creation of the dismembered humanity, ontology and cosmologies to build Africa's superpowers. In post-colonial conditions, Africans referred themselves with derogatory terms, Anglophones, Francophone, Lusophones and other terms linked to colonial experiences, and this acts as a source of sharp divisions among statesman which traumatised the anti-imperialist idea of unity, a decolonial unit. Power struggles, Eurocentric governance, petty bourgeoisie and fascist nationalist African leaders affects the existence of unity. The dream of unity envisioned by the founding fathers of Africa, strongly purified by the anti-imperialist Colonel Muammar El Qaddaffi of Libya and the late Robert Mugabe of Zimbabwe as roads to go to achieve absolute independence, however Gadhafi was murdered in the broad day light by US led

NATO (North Atlantic Treaty Organisations) over the alleged cases of human rights abuse and Mugabe was sanctioned over land reform project. Africa unite we're coming out of Babylon. Bob Marley wisdom informed by the conditions of Africans all over the world, people of color dream to see a better world, a peaceful world where people live together without uhistorical, social hierarchy and racial division of the society.

"We're the survivors, a black survival.
In this age of technological inhumanity
We're the survivors. Black survival scientific atrocity, we're the survivors
Atomic mis-philosophy, we're the survivors, nuclear mis-energy
It's a world that forces lifelong insecurity
All together now we are the survivors, yes the black survival"

From 1619 to present, black race did not go extinct, but continued to thrive. We didn't extinct from slavery, lynching, genocides, chemical biological weapons and today we continue the existence as a threat to evil, a threat to Babylon empire and its system. Black people are now consciously realizing the source of their problem and implementing the projects to unlearn racial inferiority, western epistemologies and cultures, as Buffalo soldier, uprise against the system and sing the "songs of freedom". Black consciousness, Pan Africanism, decoloniality, negritude, black power, Afro-socialism and Ubuntu, are all dedicated philosophies to the total liberation of African being, space and cosmology. We are survivors as black nation, survived from racism, colonialism and today neo-colonialism, Bob Marley was ahead of his time, a prophet to the world. For Bob Marley, decoloniality means a total liberation from mental slavery as the source of all confusions, rebuild the black

89

nation not as tower of Babel, but power of babel (Mazrui 2003), and adhere to moral principle of living together, as one through love. Therefore decoloniality as anti-imperialistic is not seeking to create an iron curtained black philosophy, but a nation beyond 'boarders' tolerating others despite of color, religion and ethnic. To him that's peace, not just an absence of war, but the present of love in multicultural tolerance and total annihilation of racism. Most people compare him with Peter Tosh and Bunny wailer, but three of them were the best pioneers of reggae, speak out about the ideal of freedom, even influence and strengthen today's Afro-jazz. Bob Marley was the icon of anti-imperialism, a freedom guitar and musical words to fight social-racial injustices. A true Buffalo soldier.

Chapter 9

Hip-Hop and Harlem Renaissance: Revolutionary Mentality from Ghetto Voices

Expressing life experiences through music, lyrics, transforms emotions in words, words into lyrics, lyrics into music to communicate, document, heal and proposing a solution to the problem. Music is as old as society, its used for various purposes but at this juncture, the author aimed at demonstrating the importance of music as anti-white supremacy and anti-colonial struggles at this moment Hip-hop is the center of discussion. Before delving much into the origin of that genre, Harlem Renaissance provides an informative frameworks of the struggle of the black cause in the modern world, which believed to be the mother of black history revolution, Pan Africanism, civil rights movements and the poetic presentation of the life situations in Hip-hop music. The relevance of Hip-Hop, a cry for freedom, a cry for justices is linked to its origins from the ghettos of New York, Harlem, Baltimore and all blacks communities, therefore voices from the ghetto were heard crying for freedom, begging for social-racial equality, mourning the collapse of black nation, crying for justice and these voices were the most innocent call for humanity, the call for re-making the society whereby all humans were treated equally despites race, sex, age and gender.

Harlem Renaissance as the most organized anti-racial movement in which black people consciously questioned the existing historic narratives and social systems linked the history of transatlantic slave trade and colonialism. Colonialism and Slavery as twin treacherous events, social systems, are the reasons of today's global structure, white as superior and blacks as inferior, is the reasons for countless civil rights movements and anti-racial struggles as to create a word accommodative to all cultures, races and sexes treated as equal human beings. Slave and colonialism participated in dehumanization project of African people, successfully established dominance and controlled all facets of life of the people of color for the hundreds of years. Five centuries of mass murder, lynching, indoctrination, inferiorization, mistreatment to the extent that white dominance claimed legitimacy and naturality to rule the black people. This situation left black people with no option but to demonstrate inferiority, as a result of realisation of this issue, revolutions orchestrated to dismantle the white supremacy. For Mignolo (2013) and Maldonado-Torres (2013) the world polarized into two, the zones of humans and zones of sub-humans manifesting, informs racial Manichaean misanthropy, dispossession and dehumanization of the people of color.

The relations of these zones is hierarchical, which basically led to the imposition of certain values by the elites to the bottom and exploitation is inevitable. Elites and peasant relation, master-servant relation, industrialist-proletariat relations mirror the image of the existing global structure originated from the history of conquest. These relations distance the relations, separates development and the intimacy is likely exploitation. White aristocracy holds the power to define; defining concepts, labels and systems. This is best described in the 'Wretched of the Earth' by Frantz Fanon (1967), describing the reflections of the experiences of peasants under colonial-capitalist society, peasants described as 'Wretched of the Earth' meaning poor people, illiterates, barbaric, non-humans and subject to exploitation as well as brain washing programs implemented through law enforcement agents, media, law and education. The epistemological foundation of this argument is based on the critical thinking of how relations came after transatlantic slavery were owned, branded as animals and forced to work for long hours, mistreated and those who showed resistance gruesomely murdered in front of other black folks to send the message of terror and fear as political strategy to cripple revolution, even the religion used to calm resistance in slave plantations. After the abolishment of slavery and during colonial times the aspect of 'us and them' separates the two races' home of resistances, blacks relegated to the ghettos.

These ghettos were havens of crimes, violence, thug life, gangster life, prostitution and drug abuse, but these people transact to the existing environment of white supremacy, denied equal employment opportunities, equal wages, opportunities to learn as the strategy to enforce dominance. These were tertiary parts of slavery, embracing mental slavery and totally brainwash Afro-Americans. As a result of this highest stage of slavery and dehumanization, the cultural residues and color differences act as the starting point of questioning the history of the Afro-American people, their connection to African roots, culture and spirit. Haiti revolution and the cultural-spiritual consciousness of the Afro-Caribbean re-ignites the wide spread political and intellectual movement which resulted in Pan-Africanism and the famously known civil rights movements. The notion of black people, as people without history, inferior race and misinterpretations of Bible questioned as part of the revolutionary movements against the solipsistic racial dominance of the white race in all spheres of life. George G.M James, John Henrick Clarke, Garter G Woodson to mention a few played the most illustrious role in redefining African history, Afro-American history and great civilisations along river Nile, Niger river, River Kongo, Zambezi River and Limpopo river.

These reflections of critical thinking act as the most important stages of threatening the existing mental slavery, broaden and restructure black studies, Africana Studies or Afro-American Studies in history clubs and school using in Afrocentric (Asante 2006). For instance George G.M. James wrote about the stolen artefacts from the Egyptian mystery and the library of Alexandria, whereby Thales, Socrates, Democritus, Anaximander, Aristophanes and Hypocrates schooled by the Egyptians. Aristotle together with Alexandra the Great stole philosophy from Egyptian library at Alexandria. This is proven by the lack of accuracy in the date, location and authorship of the Greek philosophies and in most cases the accounts of their stay in Egypt. Therefore, Greek civilisation was used as the starting point of European or western civilisations, one cannot write or talk about the western civilisation without giving reference or acknowledging Greek civilisations, the concepts of medicine, mathematics, logic, philosophy and physical science, however, one cannot give an objective argument without acknowledging Egyptian philosophy, black Egyptian. The Memphite theology, laws of Ma'at, Egyptian geometry, philosophy, architecture plagiarized by Greek philosophers. Diop (1974), Asante (2006), Joachanan (2000) and Obenga (2004) supports this idea with empirical evidence based on Radio Carbon Dating, Archaeological excavation, and linguistic analysis and Hieroglyphics interpretations.

Carter G Woodson also participates in Harlem Renaissance by introducing black history week envisioned to teach Afro-Americans about Africa's past, he discovered the miseducation of the black people as the source of confusions which ensnared black minds in the ghettos and margins. Afrocentric consciousness invented to counter Eurocentric narratives of the African history was designed to justify the continuous slavery, forced labor and colonialism as the best for Africans to bring them to light, recue them from barbarism, but the point is slavery and colonialism vandalizes African glory, Afrocentric consciousness based on re-member the dismembered to create an environment useful to transact as to influence behaviors, community consciousness, black solidarity, restore black aesthetics and refuel revolution towards equal rights in the United States. The civil rights movements came into being led by non-violence movement by Martin Luther King Junior and the radical movement led by Malcom X. Most people misunderstood this fact Martin Luther King Junior and Malcom X were not opponents, but fought racism in different way, civil disobedience and radicalism. Marcus Garvey, WEB DuBois, George Padmore as products of Harlem Renaissance transforms Pan African philosophy into reality through back to Africa dream, were the role models and inspired wider scale anti-racial movements in Africa and America.

From the US media, black communities images and thuggery life presented which act as the dehumanization strategy, but in that thuggish environment new form of civil rights movements emerges different to that of 1960s US ghetto uprisings but similar to that of Caribbean anti-colonial spiritual movement based on music, reggae music. Hip-hop activism as youth music revolution characterised by rhymes, poetic lyrics mainly talked about the life situation in the ghetto, escape alternatives. Afro-American history, slavery, mental slavery and speak about the rights of black people. The genre emerge from the unemployed youth, poor youth and the victims of racism transformed their emotions into music and told the world about the realities of Blackman's experiences in the USA. It was hip hop activism that influenced mob uprising, Black Nationalism and nourished "Black Panther' spirit of revolutions around 1970s and 1980s. 2pac Shakur rose into prominences and arguably the best hip-hop artist of all time directs his lyrics to how the white supremacy system continued to dehumanize black people in the USA. The main arguments of the artist was to spread the works, to teach the people and instill the mentality of changing the oppressive world. He became the voice of the voiceless, standing for truth, speaking against police brutality, injustices, racial inequalities and subjugation of the black people. He died in 1996, but his music is still relevant today, and inspires numerous hip-hop artist for justice and sing for truth.

These hip-hop artists transact to the old system environment of systematic racism and the waves of revolutions, therefore Hip-hop activism constitutes the voice of the oppressed speaking for Justice, truth and black pride. Though hip-hop touch other facets of life, sometimes used demeaning languages, "I am a hoe, a bitch, mother fucker" (Cress-welsing 1991), but the other side of it is revolutionary, anti-white supremacist and anti-racial struggles. Kendrick Lamar is also one of the hip-hop artists of the white supremacy systems and increases in police brutalities. Hip-hop is a subculture of Afro-American arts, aesthetic and critical thinking to challenge the old institution of racism and white supremacy. Its

96

offshoot of Harlem renaissance. The constructed images of ghetto, people think of ghettos as haven of crimes, drug life, thuggery, these social pathologies are actually psychologically imposed ways of life by the system which marginalises the people as an alternatives, crowded and high density of people interactions into something good out of ghetto, music and art is the good example, therefore for not to forget Hip-Hop in the ghettos.

/

Chapter 10

Wakanda: Filming African Images

Black Panther movie, written and directed by Ryan Coogler depicts African historiography, heritage and futuristic aspects of the African Continent if it fully delink herself from the western empire and rediscover the lost self. The image of Wakanda, a fictional city created by Stan Lee Kirby raises a lot of questions, depicts image of colonial-exploitation free Africa, reconnects the glory of the ancient states to present day. In this essay, Wakanda is Kemet, Timbuktu, Great Zimbabwe, Shangay, Oyo and other great ancient cities rediscovered, the author stop the night of colonialism and remember the past glory of Africa to remake the present. An imaginary view of Africa's uncolonised, a continent never exploited or colonised, therefore it is a worth fictional story to re-imagine Africa's glory and de-mythologizes Africa as continent without history, people without soul and barbarians". The fictional state prove the Eurocentric interpretation of history wrong.

The location of Wakanda, its relevance to modern day politics of imagination, cultural representation Afro-American-Africa relations, scholastic inventions, politics and resource administration are the main themes to be exploited in this essay to delve into the depth ages of the epistemic issues surrounding Wakanda imaginary senses. Wakanda is an independent African states where its location is debated and centered among scholars. Subrick (2018) concurs that, political economy of Wakanda represents that of Botswana, a state rule and economically developed country that embraced its diamond deposits, but his depiction was imaginary not empirical since the country is also an imaginary fiction. For Ta Nehisi Coates,

Wakanda is located on Lake Victoria, near Mahannda, Canaan, Azania and Niganda, mostly in real life is the Eastern half of the Democratic Republic of Congo (DRC). Some scholars believed that, it is located in Lake Turkana, in between South Sudan, Uganda, Kenya supported by the theory of language, Hausa as one the dominant central eastern and western Africa. However, director Ryan Coogler stated that his depiction of Wakanda in 2018 Film Black Panther was inspired by the Southern Africa Kingdom of Lesotho; language, culture and governance systems support this verdict. For instance Xhosa language which is dominant in the South Africa.

This is an ongoing debate about the location of Wakanda, but to discover the new terrains of arguments the Egyptians Empire depicted by the Wakanda fiction, issues of technology, Egypt was far much ahead in terms of technology, geometry, architecture, philosophy and intellectual system. Wakanda architecture is a modernized Egyptian architects. T'Challa character depicts Egyptian pharaohs such as Ramses, the tribes and the Royal Family exemplifies Egyptian civilisation. Apart from Egyptian argument, Wakanda can be a depiction of strong West African States such as Timbuktu due to its wealth from mineral deposits, international relations with American and European states in trade. The intellectual development and strong organisations depicts the old Malian Empire. However, the warrior herded of people of Wakanda and the leader depicts the old Great Zimbabwe, Munhumutapa and Rozvi Empires which resist Portuguese colonialism for centuries and built unique cities, different from the modern popular European architecture. Mineral and resource management, spiritualism and cultural cosmologies depicts the old

Shona civilisations, sustained by the discovery of minerals deposits, gold, copper and iron. However, Wakanda is an example of African past kingdoms, traces the history, rewind it and skip colonialism, it was a depiction of African today, If the continent had not been affected by slavery and colonialism, Africa will be far much ahead of civilisation. The theatrical presentation of Africa history is not just for entertainment but as a system of spreading the truth about Africa, debunking Eurocentric historical monologue and restore black pride. The coming of the movie Black Panther celebrated African heritage, challenge the existing broadcasting of Africa history present in Eurocentric media.

"The symbolic importance of this fantastical African nation, untouched by slavery or colonization and filled with black images of grandeur, cannot be overstated. Our romanticised vision of what Africa could have been had the continent not been brutalized for capitalist gain-or what black people could be in a world free from white supremacy-is the Wakanda Dream" (Eschmann 2018)

Wakanda have symbolic importance, imagining the continent free from brutal oppression of white supremacy and the possibility of its civilisation, architecture, and culture and governance system. It is a strong imagination which cultivates black pride and confidence to fight white supremacy in media and social realities to reclaim the lost ontologies. The project was part of decolonising the mind. Wakanda has six tribe, the merchant tribes, the mining tribe, the merchant tribes the Jabari village, Burnin Zana (Golden City), the Vebranium Mound and Burtise. Wakandan people speak Wakandan, Xhosa, Hausa and African English. In terms of language as unifying factor, Hausa and African English used as medium of communication in inter-ethnic communication since these are communalist languages like Kiswahili, Hausa and African English played a most important role in promoting unity. Instead of being a tower of Babel, it is a power of Babel (Mazrui 2001).

Malken (2018) argue in relation to city planners whereby Wakanda civil, architectural and city planning design is more realistic and defined as the future. Infrastructural models and technology holds futuristic imagination of architecture and art designing, but it is uniquely African, a modified Pyramids and Egyptian cities, urban-cultural center like Timbuktu, modernized Ethiopian Empire, and its city planning resemble the Great Zimbabwe State. Wakanda is pure Afrocentric urban design, influences the African artistic renaissance of city planning and architecture different to modern Europe. Therefore, it imagines the society untouched by colonialism and slavery. Egypt conceive all global civilisations (Diop 1974, Sertima 2002, Joachanan 2008), what if it was not conquered by the Arabs, Greeks, Romans and British, what would it be like today? In BCs it was far much developed than Europe in the 15th Century, hence the depiction of glorious Wakanda civilisations re-telling the story of Africa's birth place of humanity and civilisation and imagining the presence Africa if the continent was untouched by colonialism.

Wakanda spiritual cosmology was connected to its monarch, cultural values, kinship and theology, the fiction depicts the deity or theological system present today in Africa which is ancient. Mbiti (1966) (Wiredu 2002) opines that, Africans were more spiritual than religious and communication to God was through spirit mediums, ancestors and cultic priest, the decisions of war, juristic judgment and coronation of new king were divinely influenced as to promote ethical-moral practice of the leaders, respect by the people and justice. The influences of deity as highest being and the final decision maker in social and political affairs. In Wakanda set up, people have the authority but power is vested on the Supreme Being, God, shows the strong bond between religion and politics. Wakanda deities include, Panther Goddess, based on Bastet the ancient Egyptian deity. The fictional story of Wakanda respects the existence of woman in society, as war generals, warriors played a most important role in decision making. This also evidenced by the existence of Goddess, a feminine deity as a system of balance, depicts the system of balance in ancient Memphite theology, gods and goddess played an important role in human creations, demonstrating mutual existence of male and female as the order of the society. Ancient African societies were not patriarchal in European sense, man and woman complement each other in social and political realities. Therefore, it is a call for remembering the dismembered Africa.

White gorilla cult worshipped by Jabari tribe, known for worshiping gorilla cult, Ghekre cults based on the Baoule deity of the same name and Yaoundé deity. Lion cult, Selkmet the Lion Goddess and crocodile cult were among the deity worshiped by people of Wakanda. Most of the cults used animals as symbols referred by European priest as paganism but the reality was appreciating the work of God in nature and also is linked to the discourse of totemism. Black Panther is monarchical government based on hereditary leadership, this monarch manage efficiently resources, promote state security through its highly trained warrior and modern weapon armed with vebranium meteor. Its military prowess is shown in Civil War: Captain America (2016) and Avengers: Endgame (2019), fighting against the species from galaxies and protecting the earth, its vebranium dollar have value than any other currency. The depiction of Wakanda state, original Africa, dismisses the claim of Africa as people without history, without writing, without development and without technology. European colonialist such as Trevor Hugh Roper dismissed the historical existence of Africans, but the Europeans remove Africans from history through slavery and colonialism. If Africa was not removed from history, today it will be like Wakanda.

" The one who controls the media, controls the world" said Chomsky (2016), transcending to the contemporary cosmogony media controlled by the West and its global companies such as Google, Facebook, CNN and other broadcasting corporations is a strategy to consolidate Eurocentric hegemony. The stories presented on the meta-narratives project broadcast the one-centered story as to universalize the European being, novels, dramas and music, adopting a revolutionary strategy to deconstruct the existing meta-narratives broadcasting about African history and social injustices as part of the process of inferiorization of black being, however media pluralism deconstructs the existing socially constructed stereotypes. Black Panther movies played a most important role in confronting the westernised Eurocentric theatre, cinema and Africans unite to fight the same cause and remember the dismembered values.

Chapter 11

Blackening the Whitenised World

Today's world, black people have become powerful and occupy the influential positions in the international system. Black people begin to realize oppression and proffer alternatives to social and political problems caused by white supremacy. Therefore the world is now blackened, the most influential position known for reserved for whites people are now occupied by a handful of black people. That is an act of revolution, a strategy to reduce racism into rubbles. This essay, mandated to analyse the feasibility of blackening of the whitenised world towards emancipation of blacks, the historic legacy of Pan Africanism and Afro-Diasporian movements and what it means to blacken the whitenised world. After decolonisation, the most important event was the rise of Barack Obama to power, acting as the hope to the blacks around the world. Another historic incident is the rise of Kofi Anan as Secretary General of United Nations, which is the most influential positions in global decisions. What it means to blacken the world? Does it mean the increase in black official in public space means blackening the world? These questions helps the reader and writer to navigate on the unchartered terrains of knowledge about the discourse blackening the world.

The increase of black intellectuals, professors, students, scientist, artist and politicians act as the substantive reflection of the process of blackening the world. Does it mean blackening is replacing white people with black people in influential position in the world? This question builds the arguments in understanding blackening the world, its meaning and relevance to global peace. It is necessary to navigate on the tumultuous waters on how the world was whitenised, its effects and social-political outcomes. Most scholars refer to transatlantic slave trade as point of departure, but the land of blacks was already weakened by Arab, Roman conquest and incessant internal divisions (William 1992). The fall of Grenada 1492, the conquest of America and Valladolid Judgment exacerbates the departure of African being from history and civilisation. The world whitenised and dominated by the Aryan people, the Caucasians and dehumanized Indo-Aryans, Mongolians and black Africans through colonialism.

The reincarnation of Archimedes Alexandra the Great of Persia as Greek Ruler and Roman Emperor to dominate the world find its shelters in white race, implements it and controls it. It is a demon need to be exorcised. The methods of controlling the world are racism, slavery, colonialism, epistemicide, cultural genocides, exploitation and geopolitical world systems. These methods were embedded on the idea of white supremacy, class society of white superior-black inferior dichotomy. Race becomes class. Thus gave birth to racial hierarchy funded by the sub-humanisation and vandalisation of the sources of black pride, such as culture and history. That is to say, history falsified to the extent that black people were referred to people without soul, no historical conscience and subject to slavery and conquest as mission civilistrice. Fredrich Hegel and Champollion Fegeac famously known for disposing Africans from history, decenter the Egyptology narratives from its original Black African roots to Indo-European civilisations.

This dilemma continued, whereby in global matters black people were left outside of the modernity, global decision making and developmental praxis. At the treaty of Westphalia 1648 as the starting point of modern states, at the Congress of Vienna, Paris Peace Settlement in 1919 at the world war one and San Francisco Conference in 1945 drafts the contemporary state models, relations, governments and human rights, black people were not there and these are the most important events that shaped the modern world. For instance modern sovereignty nations templates resulted from Treaty of Westphalia of 1648 and the modern human rights discourse conceived by San Francisco Conference in 1945 and no African states was there. The dichotomy of developed-developing nations revolved under the schematic concepts of zones of being and zones of non-beings as dames or Wretched of the Earth (Maldondado-Toress 2018). Concepts, labels and systems are designed by the white race, therefore the world is whitenised, controlled by the Euro-American modernity.

Legends such as Nehanda, Chaminuka resists the whitenisation of Zimbabwe. The process of whitenising Africa was also effected through Catholicisation and christianisation of the religious space, were God and Angels whitened and the story of sons of Noah used as the origins of black people. The distortion of truth universalised to brainwash people of color and indoctrinate blacks with inferiority ideology. However, world wars vividly explains the collapse of whitenised world and reach the menopausal stage, threatened by Pan Africanism and struggle for Independence across the world. Haiti revolution and various slave rebellions in the Caribbeans was a starting point of anti-white activisms as antidote to mental and political colonialism. Fanonian Marxist approach witnessed in various transitions of labor movements into peasants revolutions in Africa. The reception of Independent African Continent in the global affairs hummer the last nail on the coffin of whitened world, black people become heads of states, head of governments, commissioners, ministers and land-industrial owners as the regeneration of Africa's empire after five centuries of colonialism. The departure of colonialism in Africa shrink the European sphere of influence and led to the collapse of famous Pax Britannica.

In academic affairs, black people professors and students increases, outnumber the former privileged white race in colleges in Africa and some part of United States and United Kingdom, most of the black professors become heads of universities and colleges. The world become blackened, black people acquired power and challenged white supremacy through academic, economics and re-sharping 'black activisms'. 21st century affected by epidemics (HIV/AIDS, Ebola and COVID-19), terrorism, democratic crisis and climate change as global challenges and the Blackman was at the center of the decisions, Kofi Anan as the Secretary General of the United **Nations (UN),** a revolutionary act of dismantling the westernization of global institutions. Barack Obama elected the President of United States of America, a first black president.

In Hollywood, greatest actors such as Denzel Washington, Morgan Freeman, Taylor Perry, Jamie Fox, Idris Elba, Ice Cube, Will Smith, Martin Lawrence, the late Chadwick Bossman, Michael B Jordan, Daniel Kaluya to mention a few dominate the universalised Hollywood arts industry and take control of it. This is a heroic move to 'black community' the blackenisation of 'Hollywood''. In music, reggae as Jamaican country music fused with Afro-beat, Afro-Jazz and Rastafarianism become popular, with intellectual lyrics, poetically expressed conceptualises being black in the world, evil of colonialism, modern Babylon system, criticised racism and advocates for revolution against the system. With its rhythmic drum beatings and unique instrumental, it steals the hearts of the world from the globalized Caucasians music. In academics the decolonial movement premised on epistemic re-generation, shows the birth of critical thinkers in Africa and beyond, academia such as Cheikh Anta Diop, John Henrick Clarke, Carter G Woodson, Frances Cresswelsing and many others challenged effectively the whitenised epistemology. Chinua Achebe, Wole Soyinka, Ngugi wa Thiongo, Dambudzo Marechera, Ngozie Chimamanda Adichie and among others developed literature, transformed it from Shakespeare centered to a multicultural perspectives. The 2018 FIFA World Cup, won by France and the majority of players were blacks, which resembles black revolutions in the fields of sports and regaining confidence to showcase their capabilities. Most of the Football Stars are blacks, Sadio Mane, Naby Keita, Ousmane Dembele, Kilyan Mbappe, Paul Pogba, and Romelu Lukaku to mention few. Brazil constitutes majority of Red Indians, Colored and Black People, up to date it dominates Football, have fantastic talents, skills and make football a beautiful game.

In analysis, everything is now blackened, the religion blackened, politics is blackened, academics is blackened, arts and entertainment blackened therefore black people now regenerates the old Kemetic glory and dominance. However, to blacken the system is not just populates the world influential sector with black people, but with black systems and mentality. This is lacking in process of blackenisation of the world, it's a black skin white mask (Fanon 1967), whereby the most alienated blacks are the one who are on top on influential positions, instead of representing black interest they joined the system, integrated in it and polishes it. The most celebrated blackenisation of the universities is meaningless to the struggle of black people, though it's a revolutionary act but the challenge is it replaced personals not systems and black academia maintain the so called global standards. But how global is those standards? If those global standards situated in Euro-American zones? Therefore, blackening the world means more than just occupation of positions, it transcend to the ideological concern of Pan Africanism, black power and Afrocentricity. It means blackening the way of thinking, aesthetic and cultural context. James Baldwin in his essay "Stranger in the Village" states that, this world is white no longer, and will never be white again".

Chapter 12

Black and Beauty: Reflections of Anti-Imperial Aesthetics

What it means to be black? How the world see black people? How black people see themselves? The relation of Blackness and beauty? These general and philosophical questions informs a critical analysis of the aesthetic study (study beauty of blackness), black magic, black intellectual production. The public sloganise 'black is beauty or black beauty' are not just phrases recited in street corners but its inherent ululation of the variables, 'black and beauty', the relation of objects and subject is a revolutionary intellectual act to define the black space and its relevance to the black people. Most of the people who used to say that are black people, why not white people? It is a process of re-imagining the world in black perspectives. Re-imagining black space through lived experiences and re-connecting with the past glory before the night of colonialism and slavery which distorted the way we see ourselves, the way we see the world in us and our relations with other races. It creates an imaginary differences belonging and leading to the existentiality "us and them" dichotomies, what is the difference and similarities, how we have arrived to that; the differences and similarities. These are critical issues in the contemporary study of politics, race and gender.

We learn to see things, meaning to say, it is a learned process to differentiate and define beauties. It is learned from the community, schools, religious institutions, media, family and the objects surrounding us, that is when human beings develop a perspective of seeing and viewing things from the different angles and have effects to social relations as well as race relations. The presentation of blackness and whiteness in the world is based upon hierarchy and the balance between positive and negative as metaphysical system. Black is represented as evil, ugly, bad and other derogatory terms but white as good all the positive terms.

> "After reading Tanizaki's essay on aesthetics "In place of Shadows" I tell this sister in a late night conversation that I am learning to think about blackness in a new way. Tazinaki speaks of seeing beauty in darkness and share this moment of insight. "The quality that we call beauty, however, must always grow from the realities of life, and our ancestors, forced to live in dark rooms, presently came to discover beauty in shadows, ultimately to guide shadows towards beauty's end" (Hooks 2010: 134)

This is how Hooks (2010) and Tazinaki (2003) chemistry started seeing beauty in the darkness, since it defines the experiences of black ancestors, locked in dark room but seeing hope and light at the end of the tunnel, sometimes ugly is beautiful is just the way we see things differs, what they call ugly to us is beauty. Post-structuralism on art, literature and aesthetic criticizes the existing meta-narratives and the imposed Eurocentric paradigms of seeing things, using Eurocentric culture and location to define the existence, intellectual discourses and labels, therefore non Europeans left outside of the creation of the meanings of the social world and to some extent deposited the certain way of thinking which led to the inferiority image of blackness. For Lezra (2016), imperialism succeeded as result of the implementation of 'demonising the other which creates an ugly image of the colonised, hence inferiority complex'. The coloniality of the black images in its social-political appearance, black bodies in its biological objectivity and black being in its existential thoughts, reflects in the descriptions of the blacks as ugly, people without soul, animalist, and people without history, humans and barbarians. Why this perspectives and modes of seeing black people?

Early Asians and Europeans travelers, the like of Herodotus, Count Volney, Greek scholars and Portuguese explorers accounts described Africans in a positive way in two perspectives, (1) the image of African bodies as dark skinned, wooly hair, broad nose, thick lips, muscular, thin waist and big buttocks they did not mention the ugliness but differences to them, the us and them concepts from the European universe. Secondly, they described African continents and its people as vast terrain of natural resources, social organisations and customs, hospitable, strong army and architecture. When black people first encounter the Europeans, they did not see a threat, a non-human or a superior being but a friend, a brother with another color and distant relative from other side of the world. However, when Europeans came with the motive to colonialise Africa and enslave them, which is when the idea of ugliness of African being erupt as a way to promote power relations based on superiority of white race. These selfish motives were central on the theological debates about the origins of human species, therefore Europeans whitenised God's image, Christianity and angels to claim universal superiority and nearness to God through their image, race as God's race.

The construction of these images distorts the way black people see themselves, existences as bodies, images and beings and their differences to the white race, dominated by the European theological and political view. The way blackness presented in

112

European literature, art and epistemologies on white interest to chain black being in the whitenised prison cells. The word Negro came into being to define blacks as ugly, ape alike and the place of origins as uncivilized space. The word realties to the biological existences, similarities to animals and its relations to nature, this uncivilized, barbarians, people without history and people without soul, all these descriptions are close to animal description in European literature. Therefore in colonial times, slavery, post-slavery and the modern world, this led to continuous view of blacks themselves as representing the ugly human species, unfit to the global description of beauty transacting to the whitenised environment, the coloniality of beauty. Most of beauty contest around the world the word world, among black communities white bodies used as template of defining beauty, a mode of beauty judgments. Apart from that, the increase in cosmetic industries, black people used plastic surgery, bleach skins, straitening hair and emulated the speeches as to look like Caucasians. Coloniality, defined as dehumanization of people of global south originated from colonialism and sustained by the celebrated capitalist modernity values (Wynter 1994), hence coloniality of beauty is based on the universalization of the concepts and templates of European beauty and relegates other cultural aesthetic views of beauty, hence to be beautiful one needs to look like Caucasians. Caucasians are now figures, images and models of beauty in the global world.

This reflections of experiences vividly demonstrates the psychological impacts of colonialism, coloniality of image and being. It distorts the way we see things, everything 'black' is ugly and the concept of blackness represents ugliness in Eurocentric

113

literature and social cosmogony. We see our black bodies as curse, we are not proud of our Melanin, sexiness, bodies, thick lips and wooly hair, we always look for alternatives to change the way we look, our skins and hair and we have taught so, hundreds of years of indoctrination, exposed to Eurocentric space which always denigrates black bodies as dirty, ugly and heathen thoughts. Most of the black people accepts it as reality, of course cosmetics originated from Africa, but the way it is consumed reflects the coloniality of beauty, burning our skins to look like Europeans. Colonialism and racism helped us to shape the way we see ourselves as ugly and see them as replica of beauty. This also is aided by the materialism, the existence of wealth in European countries and lavish lifestyles.

However, melanin movement, black beauty aesthetic activism and black the father of humankind intellectual arguments, black literature and black art challenges the existing myth of the ugliness of black being, body and image in social space, aimed at restoring confidence and restructures the way we see ourselves and others in the world, what makes us different? This movements threaten the existing systematic white superiority, since the way we started to see bodies as reflection of beauty that is when black people started to break the chains of mental and imaginative slavery and global race-class. This is a breaking point of the approximately four centuries old system that left black people outside global civilisations for longtime, some of these aesthetic movements adopts radicalism of black people is beautiful and white is ugly as a result of the reflective experiences of blacks under the hands of white race from fifteenth century to present. The struggle is about differentiating "us and them" in color and aesthetics projection. To unlearn the

114

learned way seeing things and relearn the beauty the beauty of the blacks, the representations of black people in history and deconstructionist images resuscitating black people's confidence to participate in the global social, political and economic processes.

> "Keeping my natural hair shows that I am content with my looks, I appreciate my African Hair, I am beautiful with my own hair. I believe colonialism poisoned our minds and altered it to believe that only whites are beautiful hence for you should have white features such as straight hair. Afro-Hair is a way of embracing yourself. Yes I have natural hair its does not resemble poverty however it shows how strong I am. My hair can stand gravity and I can stand all obstacles as well" (Thelma Royal Machinga)

In a conversation with Thelma Royal Machinga, she alludes many factors about being beautiful and Africaness, highlights the role of colonialism in affecting the concept of beauty whereby white beings are used as a template of beauty. The aspect of Afro-Hair movement is an important Afro-beauty realisation and revolutionary aspect against cognitive dissonance.

Black beauty contest, Afro-Hair campaigns and hash-tag Melanin movements or the proud calling of "Son of the Soil" demonstrates the re-awakening of black aesthetics, erotics and creation of literature and poetry as 'spiritual movement' of the long lost black people. Afro-Jazz, Jamaican reggae and dancehall, Afro-pop, Afro-American Hip-Hop, Afro-Caribbean literature, Afro-American art, paintings and other genre of art and literature of the African and African descents in diaspora as the collective movement, recreating the aesthetic views of black bodies, image and being in the collapsing whitenised world. As people of color we must unlearn to re-learn to see the world in African standpoint, past, cultures relations and the future aspiration.

Chapter 13

Barrel of Pen and Belonging: Rewriting African History in African Perspective.

> "Philosophers have long concluded, however, that everyman has two education that which should be given to himself and the other that which he gives himself. Of the two kinds the latter is by far more desirable indeed all that which constitutes over real and best nourishment. What we merely taught seldom nourishes the mind like that which we teach ourselves" (Carter G. Woodson)

Africana movement, create a retrospective framework into self-introspective of what has been imparted into our minds are vulnerable from sub consciousness influence and ought to think and classify itself in certain ways of thinking and behavior. This aspect, the image of after life and divine society, has been created by what we learnt and the available mythical existence and Eurocentric literature. As eluded by Carter G Woodson, the educational philosophy is dialectical whereby one need to be educated by someone and also educate himself/herself. That marks the beginning of modern schools, colleges and universities. In this regard, that education system is more privileged. What really constitutes that education system? What one may teach him? What kind of information one someone may teach? This question enable one to revisit the archive of my book titled *"Phenomenology of Decolonizing the University; Essays of Contemporary Thoughts in Afrikology"* which I wrote during my final year at the university. Summarised in that way, university education embrace Eurocentric approach that promotes the universalization of western values and continue to chain the minds of people of the South, hence that education system need to be decolonized since it is a manifestation of colonialism. The main thrust of this chapter is about writing Africa of my ancestors, using the knowledge I have been taught and learnt from my prestigious university, which is home and what I have taught myself during the course of my undergraduate studies at Midlands State University. It is of best interest to me to venture in the writing of my fatherland, the land of my ancestors as to speed up the project of knowing my self-and decolonization. Anthropology, Political Science, Philosophy, Sociology and other disciplines literature dominated by Eurocentric thoughts, hence we need to redefine knowledge system through writing our own narratives, with our own approaches

The sense of belonging in African community which I came from, knowledge making has no individual ownership. Which hardly convince myself that African knowledge manifest itself in cosmos based on I am because we are philosophy. The senses of belonging, extended to epistemic domain, the self-defined by the society. Literally means, myself defined by society I live. The case of modern generation, the identity crisis invites an enormous attention of various scholars of African Studies. But the pen, in whose story and approach? Continuity on assessing the art of belonging and fodder the sense of belonging to present and future generation's documentation of orature. Stories that we were used to be told by our elders under the moonlight, encircling fire as kids. Some of those stories have animal characters such as Baboon, Hare, Tortoise and Elephant as satire, to spice up the comedy. However there were not just general stories but tales with deep history, inviting listeners to have critical minds and imagining the past and reinvent the mythical belief of the world. Listening to those stories it equips the minds to know and to be curiously searching about the past, which I Call "Africa of My Ancestors". The book titled "Rethink African Being; Debunk Eurocentric Historical Monologue (Decolonial Epistle II) explains the methodologies and approaches of researching for truth and rewriting African history. Which is an assignment to complete, as to venture in preservation of our own narrative, with glorious past not wilderness as it is claimed by Eurocentric Historians. The aspect of Ngano (Folklores) has been embraced arguably by Ignatius Mabasa as one of the most important issue in children's literature and Rethink African storytelling and writings. The narratives by Shona novelist such as A M Hamutyinei, Ignatius Mabasa, Patrick Chakaipa and Felix Mugugu just to mention a few. Those cultural narratives relay the button stick of developing Shona literature and shaping the society in the called post-humanistic society. African cultural writing consciousness is the key necessary movement to pen and shape African society, since it will be a dominant literature in the so called schools and universities that fed the aspect of belonging and identity. Writing Africa of My Ancestors, through documenting folklores re-center 'Africa' in the so-called intellectual society that reduces the gap between African home knowledge and the so-called schools. In present situation, African homes give best education to children, mainly aided by the role of 'home professors'-mothers, nature children, taught them values that influence their thinking and understanding their sense of identity.

"Our females must be qualified because they are mothers of our children. As mothers are the first nurses and instructors of children, from them children consequently get their first impressions, which being always the most lasting should be the most correct. Raise mothers above the level of degradation, and the offspring is elevated with them" (Martin Delaney).

In terms of belonging, Black Nationalist Martin Delaney quoted by Tolagbe Ogunleye-explain the national making of black society, including the role of woman in identity making, which later I develop in the theory "De-Sexism". Woman plays the most important role in identity making, mainly on the aspect of storytelling. My experience with my 'home professors' also corroborates this issue. The mind of Africaness drilled in me every day at moonlight gathering, encircle the late Matilda Chitsinde and Juliana Kapuya, narrating stories about the past, belief of the universe and the myth where we come from as a society, a clan and a nation. Are those stories gone forever? I was challenged by those great 'professors' storytellers and induced the sensation of writing Africa of my ancestors. I begin with a theory of decolonizing the university, offloads historical monologue and the art of knowing thyself and preparing the De-sexism theory to honor home professors' shaping my thinking. Honoring Africa's past need to be documented in knowing ourselves and singing the epistemic freedom. I grew up in ghetto and rural areas, these two confrontational environments co-author my aesthetic views of life. Urban or ghetto culture represents new cultures fashioned in modern life style, and individualism. It is highly influenced by the western cultures.

However rural societies still embrace African values, and the conception of communalism. For instance, if you saw an Elder on the way you are supposed to greet him or her however contrasting with urban cultures. The conflicting issue of rurality and urbanity has been a problematic factor in doing away with colonialism, Mahmood Mandani pen "Citizen and the Subject", whereby those who are guided by civil law are citizens and those who are mainly governed by customary laws in rural areas are subjects. Hence the polarization of African society creates a bombshell to the comprehensive development of decolonial theory. The barrel of pen as battle weapon of reshaping who I am through literature, music has a major effect in liberating self, as 'African Being'. The ontology comprehension of music philosophy in shaping the society resides in its open understanding of music role in spiritual behavior. Mbira music-the deep cultural load deposited to the banks of African history in penning the history of the society. Ethnomusicology, as part of African philosophy methodology approach introduces the template of knowledge of the past, visual arts and choreographies. The meta-logic of the conception of African history revolves in the prognosis of reclaiming the past. Writing Africa of My Ancestors referred to as Dark Continent by Harvard, Cambridge and Oxford Professors. If it was a dark continent, which means there was light before and it was blown off. Who to blame? Authors of African history, employ Eurocentric historical attributes in the project of de-humanization of the black race. Some of the African historians are trained under Eurocentric scholarship hence failed to reinvent or rediscover the Africa. Thandika Mukandaire (2011) introduces an analytical concept of three generation of African scholars since independence. Struggle to reclaim black community, education across the continent used as meta-methodology in bringing justice and development to the long gone suffering black people. Scholarship programmes bred first generation of African scholars who were exempted to study abroad under education schemes in the early years of independence. After completion of study, they came back to their original land and train native scholars (Lwazi Lushaba). Second generation of African scholars went under the same scheme abroad, but stayed there and focused on their careers. Third generation of African scholars are the product of local universities, who dedicate to teach in Africa, among these scholars, first generation of African scholars include Claude Ake who focused on explaining colonialism as economic and political force, that was credited as problem by Asante (2007). Since they engage in Marxist explanation of economic problems of post-independence society. The Eurocentric scholarship influences their thinking and some of them use mainstream discipline approaches in analyzing history and philosophy. For instances, those who were trying to justifying African philosophy failed as a result of using Eurocentric approach in defining African philosophy, However there were dedicated cadres. First generation of African scholars soon realize the new concept on manifestation of colonialism as a result of happening of new thoughts and new events, such as conflicts and the question of power politics in Africa. Scholars such as Mahmood Mandani, realize overwritten of Marxist approach to the manifestation of colonialism, hence introduce the conception of dialectic philosophy in the study of African social science.

The new methodology analysis on the issues of African society, elucidated in 'Citizen and Subject' as an explanation of social effects of colonialism and the reason for social and political divisions in post-colonial Africa. Third generation of African scholars learn and influenced by the writings of Molefe Kete Asante, and they tried to reclaim the legacy of Africa in redefining Africa. Scholars such as Lwazi Lushaba, has been in massive project as to reinvent the lost soul, the lost continent in terms of literary publication. However the work lack a pragmatic conception. Yes there are brilliant ideas such as the erudition of works of Professor Sabelo Ndhlovu Gatsheni but social engagement remain a critical factor to spearhead the idea of knowing yourself. Ancestral scholars such as Cheikh Anta Diop, Ivan Van Sertima lead in the spiritual journey to produce African literary text, which include African consciousness in the making. Dehumanization of the blacks was mainly on denialism policy, the history denied. However the rise of African consciousness based on African Agency in analyzing life style of the society unfolds the new era of thinking, regenerate a new template of epistemology in social science studies. As authors of history, I believe the aspect of integrating the royal entourage of African history is in better position to history that was denied by Eurocentric Anthropologist and Historians. Mazrui (1986) mention the importance of history, the denial of African history sub-humanizing African society, to the extent that their civilization denied the Africoid pedigree and DNA.

Ancient cities of Ethiopia, Timbuktu, Mapungubwe, Madzimbabwe and Kemet connected to Greeco-Roman and Arab-Judaic civilization was this a true view of African past? A major assignment of us African scholars is to complete, cherish the thematic approach of reconstructing our history in African standpoint, as to claim the human status in global society. Nabudere (2011) argue that African epistemology, redefined, as Afrikology is quite useful in reclaiming and re-humanizing Africa.

In spirit of Afrikology, the African society history, include the paradigm of Africanity in reclaiming the lost ontologies. Africanity in a paradigm based on writing African issues influences by social change, based on revolution. Explaining Africanity, Cabral argue that white people claim they brought us into history, but they diverted us from history, hence revolution is a necessity in reclaiming our history. Revolution defines the nature of the society in re-humanizing Africans, literature revolution is a game to change the conceptions and it unfolds new historical narratives. Though the discourse lack consciousness, it is useful in claiming ourselves as Africans, but we need consciousness. Cheikh Anta Diop (Asante, 2016 and Clarke, 2015) use African Agency in claiming the history of Egypt as part of Africa like Rome and Greece to Europe. Afrocentric theory is a conceptual framework and theoretical paradigm in redefining African self and re-claiming the lost ontologies(s).

> "Afrocentric is therefore a consciousness, quality of thought, mode of analysis, and an actionable perspective where Africans seek, from Agency, to assert subject place within the context of African history" (Asante, 2007: p16).

It is a consciousness, that include realization, questioning and hypothesise of one's being in the world or the issue of belonging. As consciousness, it applies the development of unique epistemology in analysing African issues in the fountain of African Agency. African agency includes the re-centering of African philosophy and thoughts in Analyzing black cosmogonies. Remember the metaphysics and ontology analysis, within the context of African past. Afrocentric as antonym of Eurocentric, create avenues of self-consciousness.

Broadening the space of literature's geopolitical influences the pragmatic notion of knowing yourself through literary publication. Writing Africa of my ancestors should not be limited and enclosed to the university walls, but influence the daily family and community events in the society. The dwindling of orature and folklore lessons should be replaced by meaningful literature to reclaim our identities. History and literary texts are significant in the affluent deposition of epistemology of self in contemporary society. Afrikology, Africanity and Afrocentric paradigms are significant in the reclamation of re-humanization of African identities.

Chapter 14

Rebranding My Identity: African Being in Post-Traditional Society

My identity is as a living being not belonging to myself, but to a larger community, a family, a clan and a nation. However numerous incidents happen to destroy my identity. It is difficult now to define myself as an African, in which I pose the question, "Do Africans Exist? This question invites a slogan not an answer, NO. Literally means it is a clear morphology that the DNA of identity of Africans has been long gone buried in the Sahara desert. '*Re*' branding identity, meaning to reclaim the lost identity that was plundered by the western imperialism and us Africans as victims of Eurocentric living standards. We tend to believe that everything African is traditional, primitive and nuanced that creates a success scene of the demeanment of our own identity. People raise argument-referencing modernity, which they use as a synonym of Westernism and African culture viewed as primitive way of life. The main argument about this issue revolves in misconception of culture, as permanent as unchanging template in human sociology, which is not true at the first place. Ethno-philosophers try by all means to rediscover African philosophy (John Mbiti, Placide Tempels), find positions of it into mainstream politics however their methodology invites numerous criticisms since it views African culture and philosophy as unchanging discourse. Professional Philosophers (Kwasi Wiredu, Henry Odera Oruka and Pauline Hauntondji), integrate ethno-philosophy methodology and professional methodologies and therefore find out that African cultures are dynamic like any other culture, change from time to time and are influenced by any global event.

In this regard, people failed to reimburse the understanding of African ontology, as dynamic culture and to be modern doesn't mean westernize. Chabani Manganyi (1974) once wrote "Being-Black In the World" a classical masterpiece of identity and 'systematic' racism, whereby most black Africans try by all means to run away from their identity, that creates divide and rule and structure racial superiority. This conception gave birth to the issue of inferiority, whereby due to identity crisis we failed to unite and realize that we belong to a communal philosophy of life. Malcom X refer House and Field Negro, whereby the former are the most comfortable and try to imitate the Whiteman and end up creating the other, or a sellout in black revolution. The later always thinks of cultural unity of blacks as slaves and need to revolt, but the confusion and disjuncture between house Negros and Field Negros create massive tribulation in revolution.

Re-discover Afrikology: An Epistemology and Theory Of African Being

Epistemologies, defined as branch of philosophy focus on the logic and metaphysics of knowledge as a way of life and influence human activities in the daily basis. The reflective way of life, defined about how people define themselves as humans? How they declare their belonging in global cosmogonies and claim property rights of any cartography or land? And also how they define nation, morality and kinship? All these questions remain an important issue in the quest of understanding the episteme of every society, and constitute the main anatomy of a civilized world. As Africans, Chabani Manganyi

(1974) worried about how the world treated us through the ideology of systematic racism whereby black were represented as bad omen or contempt. Hence we blacks were regarded as people without intelligence, as well as without history, hence the pride of our identity was lost in the making of new global order based on "Westerncentrism". Westerncentrism a theory explains the logic of metaphysical analysis of global society based on the values of particular place only, universalize it, which is European. It is used interchangeably with Eurocentric approach. Afrikology, an intellectual aspect in redefining Africa, is a template of epistemology connected with the roots of Africa and knowledge systems. It is an offshoot of Afrocentric theory, and at Temple University is a degree programme proposed by Professor Molefe Kete Asante. Afrikology is a transdiciplinary study in African issues such as culture, architecture, history, sociology, anthropology, political science, philosophy, business and science. Its main aim is to produce consciousness in the domain of understanding Africa. Consciousness paradox a discourse in the reclamation of lost identities in the journey to so-called post-traditional society. There's a metaphysical locality connection between knowledge and the African continent that conceive Afrikology as academic discipline as a template of knowledge in African society. It inherits Afrocentric approach of consciousness and centric perceptions in imagining world, and remembers the dismembered in defining African Identity. Dani Wadada Nabudere refers Afrikology as template of knowledge in African society, which justifies the existence of African philosophy and other philosophies.

"Afrikology is not African-centric or Afrocentric. It is a universal scientific epistemology that goes beyond Eurocentrism, or other ethnocentrisms. It recognizes all sources of knowledge as valid within their historical, cultural or social contexts and seeks to engage them into a dialogue that can lead to better knowledge for all. It recognizes people traditions as fundamental pillars in the creation of such cross-cultural understanding in which Africans can stand out of having been the fore-bearers of much what is called Greek or European heritage as fact of history that ought to be recognized because from this fact alone, it can be shown that cross cultural interactions has been a fact of historical reality" (Nabudere, 2011; 92).

The conceptual understanding of Afrikology as template of knowledge in universal understanding take its roots on historical fact of Africa as cradle of human kind and all civilization. Though Asante (2007) argue that Afrocentric is not an ethno-valorised paradigm like Eurocentric, but it claims African agency in viewing Africa in particularism, that act as far much above of "Yurugu" and Africanity. However Afrikology came to strengthen theories by Runoko Rashidi, George James and Cheikh Anta Diop in historical consciousness in the origins of intellectual heritage, as owed to Africa a distinct metaphysics. In contemporary society, it works hand in glove with multiculturalism and polycentricism. Since the world has become a village, which means back to communal past remembered in global making system. However Afrikology, as template of knowledge in the society nurses Afrocentric approach in black consciousness, as philosophy and political movement in claiming identity space of Africans.

Black consciousness, a melanin revolution that shows the relation between skin color and mentality, the experience created is the phenomenological understanding of Africans as objects, and subject in global cosmology. Steve Bantu Biko, owe the principle of decolonizing the mind from Frantz Fanon (Ngugi wa Thiongo, 1985) and the principles of black revolution by Marcus Garvey. Black Skin justified as the original skin and a symbol of superiority creates the mentality of liberating blacks from mental slavery, and rethinking the identity. Mind, liberated from mental slavery through programming what is African, to renew the identity. The university walls, is a prison of African epistemology, mummifying it. It started with the coming of Arabs and later on the establishment of transplant institutions such as Fourah Bay College, Yaba College, and Makerere University, whereby teaching system was wholly Eurocentric. However decolonizing the university, help us to rediscover ourselves as African being. Afrikology, the most important template of knowledge in politics of knowing but need to be sustained by social activism, as proposed by Maldondado-Toress (2016). Social activism includes spirituality, commonness, and solidarity and rediscovers the self. That is evidenced by Black Nationalism, civil rights movements, decolonization, black consciousness, wars of liberation struggle and Fees Must Fall movement, and yield results of black unity and aid the religious movement of decolonial evangelism. This aspect is a great solution in rediscovering African being in post-traditional society. Epistemology as the basic aspect of culture defines nation and society and contribute to the self-definition of individual or society. Every society. Has its own unique epistemology, and it is a presumptive cognizance of identity as the metamorphosis of epistemology and ontologies to create an avenue of understanding different societies.

Epistemology midwife culture to create a nation. Archie Mafeje believed that, ancient social formation and identities was resultant from human interaction and the creation of common rules, kinship to govern them. A nation consists of people with same history, culture and language. In rebranding Africans and rediscovering African self to my belonging, culture and epistemology are the most important progenitors. What does it mean to be African? This question is the most important in episteme development of Afrikology and African theories. Africa defined as continent, a continent with rich history of black people from antiquity to present. The magnificent civilization of Kemet, Neolithic civilization and other civilizations that gave birth to African heritages such as ethnic, language and architecture. It is the land of black people though as a result of Arab connection and colonialism, the continent is now multi-racial. In defining one as African, it is resultant from Africaness appreciation of the roots, culture and perspective in the global world; hence in rebranding our identity the conception of history and culture is the most important aspects. Amilcar Cabral once said, revolution is the creature of culture, since he deeply understand the role of culture in uniting and fighting the common cause. It is culture that gave us identity, to be 'Zimbabwean" its culture, to be African is a result of culture. So where else can we go to define our self without culture? Since we lost our culture through escapist European values, we lost the identity. Do Africans Exist? The answer is no as a result of cultural erosion that left huge ditches and gullies in African cosmogonies.

This issue has been a clear factor to the death of African culture on the altars of Catholic Parishes. Language has been betrayed. We need to reclaim those lost ontologies to make our identities and

131

enjoy the fruits of decolonization. Ali Mazrui (1986) once said, "to know yourself is the beginning of wisdom", hence culture gave us an identity and epistemology of ourselves as people (civilized beings). Culture creates the development of intellectual heritage, like the passing on of stories of the universe, fiction and history. However, since our culture is lost, our history is also lost as well as become dark history, Africa experiences the period of intellectual vacuum from Arab conquest to colonialism. However European historians says Africa is a continent without history. Amilcar Cabral objects that kind of thinking as racist and complete misunderstanding of History.

> "Colonialist are used to saying that they have brought us into history, today we are saying that not. They have brought us out of history, our own history to follow them on their train, in the last place on the train of their history" (Amilcar Cabral)

In this regard, it is irrational to think that our forefathers were primitive and historical unconsciousness. However Amilcar Cabral reject the view. In this regard, history as the creature of culture is the main methodology in the development or rediscovering African identities.

Conclusion; Towards an African Ethnicity

Identities are the most fundamental principles in African governance issue of post-colonial trajectory. The current socio-economic and political crisis resulted from identity crisis, whereby neo-tribalism supplant the laws of continental identity, bred from our pre-colonial society. Divide and rule tactics has been problematize peace in post-colonial Africa, as a result of coloniality

132

of boundaries, however rethink our Identity of Africa universe is the key important issue in the development of ideal society. Yes our tribal identities are most important, but Africa is bigger than those narrow tribes were individuals victimized by colonial mentality boasted off.

"My point is that only Identity for the African is the tribe. I am Nigerian because a white man created Nigeria and gave me that Identity. I am black because the white man constructed black to be as different as possible from his white skin. But I was Igbo before this white man came" (Chimamanda Ngozie Adichie)

Towards an African Ethnicity, structured in the conception of Sankofa, back to the roots from present ontologies. African identities mainly about states are created at the Berlin Conference, societies divided and organic nation ceased to exist. In this regard, Africa need to rethink herself a move towards an African Ethnicity, which is defined by experiences, aspirations and culture. An African ethnicity is the large ethnic group composed of micro-ethnic society to formulate a huge united continent. The problem with African unity is the issue of colonial concept and identity crisis. Revaluing Ubuntu in the making of Pan African projection, promote the existential philosophy of Ubuntu, based on "I am because we are" shows a shared responsibility of identity and communal belonging that was an identity of peace and moral preservations. In defining us as Africans Ubuntu governs our reflective way of life, which act as the ingredient in creating one ethnic society, as to define ourselves as Africans. Reengagement in spirituality, write our stories anew in Afro-centeredness approach reshape our identity. Towards an epistemic freedom, our minds need to compose the hymn of Epistemic Freedom, to free our minds.

> "Does it means I was very neurotic,
> When I smoke the seeds of western culture, which was too narcotic,
> Hallucinates me with western names, thinking and worship,
> A song transcend into my mind,
> With traditional acoustic,
> Communal composers sing, singing epistemic freedom
> (Kapuya, 2018, presented at Midlands State University Cultural carnivals)

Singing an epistemic, an aesthetic methodology in rebranding our identities as Africans, and recreating an identity beyond colonial boarders, an African ethnicity. African ethnicity, a redemptive concept in the understanding of us as belongs to a moral society. To know myself, enable me to control the environment and unlock the capabilities within me that is the reason why the African ancestors place that principle among cardinal principles of reflection of life.

Chapter 15

No More War: *Decolorising*, Decoloniality and Liberation of the Soul in 21ˢᵗ century.

Do we need de-colorising, decoloniality and liberation of soul to unchain the world from the man-made self-destructions? Post-anthropogenic wars are far much worse lethal than the previous centuries since there is limited physical conduct but the catastrophe is massive. Ebola, VIV/AIDS, COVID-19 and other man-made diseases claim millions of people around the world, poor class and developing countries in particular. Social scientist believe that because of poverty these diseases catastrophically affects developing countries as a result of lack of basic amenities and medical equipment. It is true since management of those cases need medical resources and modern technology however, coloniality of epistemologies and being is the chief factor leading to cultural erosion and epistemicide of natural medicines used by the past generations to cure diseases. Why past generations lived long? The general answer is, they were very consciousness about diets and medicine, but due to colonialism the culture demonised and inferiorised, people started to eat Genetic Modifications Organisms (GMO) and having chemical medicines which is toxic to blood, led to series of diseases that reduce the life expectancy.

No more war, the theme of this essay, challenging the existing warfare, nuclear battles, racism, biological warfare and epistemic struggles, therefore relate to the paradigmatic concept of decoloniality and liberation of the soul. Today world is at war, but this war is western-made and threatens the global peace, cut the last thread of humanity and shocking events have prevailed as the crisis of living together and planetary challenge. The world is now too small, reduced to global village due to technology, where Brussels is now closer to Harare, New York is now closer to Mombasa as a result of the improved communication technology which bring people together, but easy to annihilate completely therefore a call for to an end of racial, nationality and religious differences, to came together as superior species, stewards and guardians of this planet. We are the custodians of peace in this world, we should build a better place for our children, grand children and generations to come, though we have different religions; Christianity, African spirituality, Taoism, Muslims, Hinduism to mention a few, but our goal is to enjoy cosmic happiness in the peaceful world, we are different but our diversity creates a beautiful rainbow at the meeting place of sun and earth, out diversity makes us beautiful, therefore no more wars, we are for peace.

Peloponnesian wars, thirty years wars, Muslim-crusade wars, Africa's great wars, European wars, cold war, nuclear race and war on terror, psychological and socially affects humanity, cripple the vision of progress and civilisation, of course these wars are responsible for technical inventions but what if the world never experiences such savagery acts, today it will be a better place, Augustinian "City of God' full of harmony, peace and love. Human beings are not that savage, reason guides our instincts, yes we can be a state of nature for Hobbes whereby humans are greedy, and selfish, but we can learn to love since the present hatred is learned through white supremacy. Chinua Achebe once said, "People create stories and stories creates people", therefore if we construct stories to cultivate peace, it will create peaceful beings, non-savagery and peaceful social co-existence. These conditions are possible to remove war, totally in human psyche and theory of social change, the arguments looks paradisal or biblical allusions, but reason is the master of all, what makes us live as small peaceful polits/villages for thousand years can make us live in the global peace.

Fukuyama (1992) penned a book, presenting the arguments about the triumph of neo-liberal order as prerequisite for peace and harmony, declaring the end of apocalyptic world characterised by ideological contestations, dictatorship, arms race and inter-state wars. His arguments were aimed at explaining the impacts of collapse of Communism or Soviet Republic as symbol of communism after the years of ideological confrontation with U.S.A. led to apocalyptic events such as Cuban Missile crisis, post-colonial protracted proxy wars, Vietnam wars, Korean wars and various battles over communism and capitalism. Russian leaders, from Vladimir Lenin, Joseph Stalin, and Nikita Khrushchev believe in communism philosophy as the brainchild of Fredrich Engels and Karl Marx proposes the collapse of exploitations of workers and peasants by industrialist, from trade unions, workers revolution and establish scientific socialism based on equality and abolishment of private property. Mikhail Gorbachev through glasnost and perestroika policies, liberalizes power which led to collapse of Union Soviet Social Republic (USSR) and Berlin Wall as a symbol of communism (Fukuyama 1992, Huntington 1996, Magstadt 2010). Therefore, Fukuyama (1992) declare it as ends of history apply Friedrich Hegel philosophy of civilized society and the "Last Man" towards global peaceful and civilized various public intellectuals advocating for peace believe in the possibility of it through the creation of states (Treaty of Westphalia 1648), international laws and institutions (jus gentium) and international morality. These scholarship can help the world to sing songs of peace.

However, this established scholarship failed to effectively established as pragmatic concept of global cosmopolitan due to its racism logic, locality and resisted universality. Noam Chomsky (2019) argued that, the resistance of universalism either to build internationalism or extinct the planet earth, resistance must at same time tolerance and costume the inferior-superior class structures. Through neo-liberal order, the world plunged into chaos, since liberalism hijacked and politicized by the government, it failed to create the same military expedition claimed to be dedicated for the protection of human's rights and democracy. For instance, Magstadt (2010). Chomsky (2016) and Blair and Curtis (2009) argued that, "Operation Desert Storm", war on terror, Libyan questions claimed to protect human rights enforcement but at the same time grossly violated human rights, disposed people from their land, butchered millions with sanctions and war as well as vandalized heritage-cultural properties, so how does it claim to be a police state yet violates those rights in the process. Does it need human rights violations to enforce human rights? Despots in Africa and Middle East claimed to be anti-imperialism in it's noble idea resisting the universalization of Eurocentric hegemony but in the process murder citizens. This is the world today, no respect for sacred rights and cultural confrontations explodes into full scale lethal wars (1996).

> "Which cause should speak? Things look bad for Great causes of today, in a 'post-modern' era when. Although the ideological scene is fragmented into panoply of positions which struggle for hegemony, there is

138

underlying consensus: the era of but explanations is over, we need 'weak thoughts', opposed to all foundationalism, a thought attentive to the rhizhomatic texture of reality in politics too, we should no longer aim at all-exposing systems and global emancipatory projects: the violent impositions of grand solutions should leave room for forms of specific resistance and intervention" (Zizek 2008)

In defense of the last cause, Zizek (2008) discusses how big explanations like liberalism failed the world, betrayed the peaceful co-existence, therefore the criticised weak thoughts are needed to rescue the planet earth from human monstrous behaviors. For Measheimer (2001) the world is a theatre of power struggles and it is likely to remain that way, this justifies Fredrich Nietzsche view of the concept "God is dead", which specifically mean the existence of political nihilism as non-escaping political cosmology. This is evidenced by nuclear race or nuclearsim in the contemporary world, whereby countries such as Pakistan, China, North Korea, USA, Russia and European countries allegedly possesses nuclear as balance of power stratagem, offensive and defensive realism, Kenneth Waltz and Scot R Segan debated about the nuclearsim and peace, Waltz adopts a neo-realist approach by arguing that, more nuclear weapons will enhance balance of power and Segan argued on the de-neuclearisation of the world as pre-requisite to lasting peace, without fear and always be in heist for war (Waltz and Segan 1995). Scot Segan believed that, nuclear weapons must be abandoned to maintain world peace, since the protracted nuclear arms race will led to deadly war, volcanic explosion and its lava consume the earth planet, burry all the civilisations. Non-Nuclear Proliferation Initiatives remain an allusion as a result of insecurity and security threats, nuclearsim remains a hindrance factor to peace.

War on terror, sanctions, epidemics, racism, exploitation of the global South resources and international injustices are the modern warfare, challenged by Fukuyama (1992) End of History and the Last Man thesis. Western Empire, referred to Babylon by Bob Marley, Vampire by Peter Tosh, suck blood of the suffers, teach people to hurt each other on the basis of race, exploits the resources of the people, a modern holocaust in Peter Tosh song No Nuclear War. Therefore, the westrnised international law, international injustices, systematic racism and decolonising knowledge production. Decoloniality is the process of transforming colonial basis of knowledge, being and power and establishing a pluriverse template of thoughts, global south recognized in the making of global order as equal player. To preserve our planet, we need to unlearn hatred and replace it with peace consciousness, enjoy our diversity and multicultural. Today, the crises of living together is now at the deep end of world crisis, frictions between ethnic groups, religious groups and racism as order of white supremacy led to numerous death in post-cold war era, therefore a call go to re-generate our social justices towards the creation of peace, liberating our souls enslaved in material and war mongering people. "Last Man", is a civilized human being believed in the cosmopolitan structure in the 21s century generation. We are the last man to protect our planet from aggressive white supremacy which possibly extinct planet and its geography.

Chapter 16

I have a dream: Imagining Post-Decoloniality Black Nation

What will the world look like after coloniality? When Black empire achieve victory from white supremacy, does it mean it will seek hegemony in the world of power competition? Another form of radical hegemony through black supremacy? As a result of centuries of western orchestrated genocides, slavery, colonialism and coloniality, will Black people avenge or revenge? What will be the relationship between black and white people? This essay is an imaginary essay aimed at questioning the post-humus white supremacy future, black being-white being relations and the global metaphysical space. The imagining decolonial world is relevant to bring answers to the questions of post-decoloniality black nation, decoloniality scholars from the Caribbean world proposes a pluriversal world, metaphysical space defined by the inclusion of all cultural interpretations of knowledge(s), epistemic pluralism, a society where man and woman, all races and religious groups treated as equal humans to the dominant whites values. Mignolo (2013), de Soussa (2018), Ndhlovu-Gatsheni (2018), Grosfoguel (2017) and Kapuya (2020) describe the decolonial world as world free from coloniality injustices, diversity cherished as the rainbow beauty expression of the earth planet and its people. Therefore, post-decoloniality world will be possible, free from racial exploitation of knowledge, promotes global cultural thinking which possibly develops the agenda of living together in multicultural sociological schema.

From the African voices, decoloniality focused on recreating the new world includes Africans and African voices in global making of knowledge and active movement of Africa in high politics and cosmologies. It resulted from the epistemic rebellion, remember the dismembered African history and cultures. In African point of view, it is mainly concerned about Africa's involvement in global economy of knowledge, the rise of intellectual renaissance and contributes equally to global systems of thoughts through intellectual activism and decolonising the university (Ndhlovu-Gatsheni 2016). This is done through re-writing African history using Afrocentric consciousness (Asante 2007, Bessie 3003, Mbembe 2016, Chikwolo 2009), humanising the university, justifying the existence of African philosophy. Therefore, this creates an image of Post-decolonial nation championing the idea of decoloniality. Apart from African voices, Afro-American and Afro-Caribbean anti-racial activism imagining a society free from racism and mental slavery whereby truth and justice served against the historic injustices of black genocides, slavery and brutalisation in the hands of white systems. The post-decoloniality world will be constructed on three social imaginary perspectives (1) Afro-Caribbean and Native-Caribbean post-decoloniality society, 2) Afro-decolonial images of the university, society and world, and 3) Afro-American post-racism image of the world.

But, what will be the relationship between Black Nation across the world, as planetary nation and other races? The historical issues possible will shape the relations, since most of the decolonial revolutionary are radical, shaped by anger of the post-structural point of view, our thoughts, actions, behavior, speeches and identities shaped by historical, hence the interaction of the past, present and future possibly will create the grave enmity of the black nation and former oppressors. The history is more horrific, slavery

142

were people treated like animals, colonialism dispossessing people from their spiritual connection to land, epistemicide, lynching, police brutalisations, biological terrorism and exploitation of resources, those systems were more horrific to the extent that Post-decolonial anger is possible to the radical realities of history. Critics may raise questions about these imaginary world, why post-decoloniality world will be possible driven by anger of historic injustices? Why Japanese bombed by US is still silent? Why post-decolonial black nation will be like that? The post-Judeophobic Jewish state today is at peace with Germany, they let bygones be bygones. The challenge about this argument is misinterpretation of the black nation suffering, Japanese atomic bomb incidents and Hitler Anti-Semitism happened once but the world witness five hundred years of black suffering, therefore it gives a difference of post-atomic Japan or post-Judeophobic Israel to post-decoloniality. We also draw lesson from post-Carthagian Southern Europe, where it was governed by anger of the past and destroyed everything Carthagian to the extent of institutionalising slave trade to the Carthagian related races.

However, I have a dream, black people, descended from Africa and are more spiritual people therefore the search for integrity, distinct, unique and civility will overpower anger, frustration about historic injustices and transform the energy of revenge to economic development, civilisation as Martin Luther's junior dream of racial integration society. I am not trying to romanticise the future of black nation as the golden images, but the present situation of quest for integration, living together consciously, dismantling racism, holds peace and decolonial movements as humanism justified to the claim of the glorious black nation. Liberalism and

143

democracy hijacked by the western capitalist systems and failed the worlds, however dismantling white supremacy will bring peace, and therefore I travelled to the future from the Ubuntu cultural point of view as anti-thesis to racism and suggesting the futuristic glorious black nation, within and outside. The black being in their own world and the interaction of black nation and white race, the suggestions might not be true but brings new forms of debate over the issue of black history, contemporary and the future.

Bibliography

Akbar, N. (1984) *Chain and Images of Psychological Slavery*, London; New Mind Productions.

Anzaldua, G. (1987) *Borderlands/La Frontera; New Mestiza;* Aunt Lute Books

Molefe, K. A. (2006) *Cheikh Anta Diop; an Intellectual Portrait;* Los Angeles; University of Sankore Press.

_____(2003) *Afrocentricity; the Theory of Social Change,* Illinois; African American Images

_____(2007) *an Afrocentric Manifesto.* Cambridge; Polity Press

_____(2016) Decolonizing the University in Africa; An Approach to Transformation in M.K. Asante and Ledbetter, C. (2016) *Contemporary Critical Thought in Afrikology and Africana Studies,* London; Rowman and Littlefield Publishers

Bessie, S. (2003) *Western Supremacy. The Triumph of An Idea.* London and New York; Zed Books,

Brahl, L. (1923) *Primitive Mentality; Anthropology.* London; Allen and Unwin

Chukwokolo, (2009) Afrocentrism or Eurocentrism. The Dilemma of African Development. *New Journal of African Studies*

Chomsky, N. (2000) *New Horizons in the Study of Language and Mind,* *Cambridge*; Cambridge University Press

Derrida, J. (1972) *Margins of Philosophy. Chicago*: Chicago University Press

Dibash, H. (2015) *Can Non-Europeans Think?* Zed Books

Diop, A. C. (1974) *the Origins of Civilization, Myth or Reality.* Chicago; Chicago University Press

_____. (1981) *Civilization or Barbarism; An Authentic Anthropology.* Chicago; Chicago University Press

_____. (1997) *the Peopling of Ancient Egypt and Deciphering of the Meroitic Script*, Chicago; Chicago University Press

_____. (1983) *Precolonial Black Africa*; Paris; Presence Africaine.

Dussel, E. (2003) *Philosophy of Liberation*, Wipf and Stock Pub

Early, G, Moses, W.J, Wilson, L and Lefkowitz, M. (1994) Symposium; Historical roots of Afrocentrism, Academic Questions 7(2) pp44-54

Escobar, A. (2010) "Worlds and Knowledge Otherwise: The Latin American Modernity/Coloniality Research Program *"In Globalization and the Decolonial Option.* London: Rutledge

Fanon, F. (1967) "The Negro and the Language". Black Skin, white mask. Penguin

Grosfoguel, R. (2013) The Structure of Knowledge in Westernized Universities; Epistemic Racism/Sexism and the Four Genocides/Epistemicides of the Long 18th Century. *Human Architecture, Journal of the Sociology of Self Knowledge Vol 11(1)*

Grosfoguel, R. Hernandez, R and Velasquez, E. (2016) Decolonizing Westernized University: Interventions in Philosophy of Education from Within and Without, University of California.

Hauntondji, P (1997) Endogenous Knowledge; Research trails, Dakar: Edition du CODESRIA

Hetela, S. (2016) Decolonization of Higher Education; Dismantling Epistemic Violence and Eurocentrism in Europe

Hume, D. (1986) A treaties of Human Nature. Oxford. Claredon Press

Hwami, M and Kapoor, D. (ND) Neo-Colonialism, Higher Education and Student union activism in Zimbabwe. University of Alberta, Edmonton, Canada.

IItelela, S. (2016) Coloniality in our universities and we must urgently decolonize. *Mail and Guardian Africa Best Read, https;//mg.co.za/article/2016, accessed on 18 September 2017.*

James, G.G.M. (1954) *"Stolen Legacy". The Egyptian Origins of Western Philosophy*, Texas; Martino Fine Books

Kapuya, Z. (2010) *Phenomenology of Decolonising the University: Essays in the Contemporary Thoughts of Afrikology*, Chitungwiza: Mwanaka Media Publishing

Mahomva, R.R. (2014) *Pan Africanism, From Cradle, Present and Future*, Leaders of Africa Network

Maldonado-Torres, N. (2016) *Outline Ten Thesis on Coloniality and Decoloniality.*

Mandani, M. (1998) *Citizen and Subject: Contemporary Africa and the Legacy of Late Colonialism; Kampala;* Makerere University

Masisi, K. (2016) "Stripped of my Dignity and Integrity Hence I can No longer breathe".

Mazrui, A and Mazrui, A. (1998) *Power of Babel, Language and Governance in Africa,* Chicago: Chicago University Press.

Mazrui, A. (2002) *Africanity Redefined.* Chicago; Chicago University Press

Mazama, A. Ed (2003) *The Afrocentric paradigm.* Trenton; Africa World Press.

Mavhunga, P. J. (2006) *Africanising School Curriculum*: The Case of Zimbabwe

Mbembe, A.J. (2016) Decolonizing the University; New Directions, Arts and Humanities in Higher Education, Volume 15(1) 29-45

McKinney. (2017) *Language in Power in Post-Colonial Schooling; Ideologies in Practise,* New York; Routledge

Mignolo, W. (2011) *The Darker Side of western Modernity: Global Futures, Decolonial Options,* Durham; Duke University Press

Mignolo, W. (2011) Geopolitics of Sensing and Knowing On (De) Coloniality, Boarder Thinking, and Epistemic Disobedience. *Transversal Text Journal.*

Mignolo, W.D and Walsh, C.A. (2018) *On Decoloniality; Concepts, Analytics and Praxis.*

Munhande, C and Nciizah, E. (2013) 'Perpetuating Colonial Legacies; Reflections on Post-Colonial African States' development trajectories, Observations from Zimbabwe. *International Journal of Humanities and Social Science Invention. Volume 2 (11) pp10-15. Accessed at www.ijhssi.org.*

Nair, R. (2013) *Drums Beat All Night, Cape Town.* University of Cape Town Press.

Ndhlovu-Gatsheni, S.J. (2013) *Empire, Global Coloniality and African Subjectivity.* New York; Bingham

Ndhlovu-Gatsheni, S.J. (2013) *Coloniality of Power in Post-Colonial Africa; Myths of decolonization,* Dakar; CODESRIA

Ndhlovu-Gatsheni and Siphamandla, Z. Ed (2016) *Decolonizing the University, Knowledge Systems and Disciplines in Africa,* Kent: Carolina Academic Press.

Oruka, O. H. (1990) *Ethics, a Basic Course for Undergraduate Studies.* Nairobi; Nairobi University Press

Oruka, O. H. (1998) *Sagacious Reasoning,* London; P Lang

Prah, K. (2009) African Languages, African Development and African Unity. Lagos; Centre for Black and African Arts and Civilization.

Prah, K. (2016) Creating Knowledge in Africa; *School of Human and Social Science Annual Lectures, University of Venda 18-20 May 2016*

Quinjano, A. (2000) Coloniality of Power and Eurocentrism in Latin America, *International Sociology, volume 15 (2) pp215-232*

Raewyn, C.S. (2016) Decolonizing Knowledge, Democratising Curriculum, *University of Johannesburg.*

Reed, W.E, Lawson, E.J and Gibbs, T. (1997) Afrocentrism in the 21st Century. *The Western Journal of Black Studies Volume 21 (3) pp73-79)*

Riskers, E. (2012) what is Decolonization and Why Does It Matter. International Cry. *A Publication Centre for World Indigenous Studies*, accessed on https//intercontinental cry. Org accessed on 18 September 2017.

Sausa, S. B. (2014*) Epistemologies of the South; Justice against Epistemicide*, London; Routledge.

Sartre, J. P. (1968) *No Exit and Three Other Plays, Dirty Hands, The Files Respectful Prostitute*, New York; Vintage Books

Sertima, I. V. (2003) *Before Columbus. The African Presence in Ancient America*, Washington; Random House Trade paperback

Spivak, G. (1994) *Can Subaltern Speak. Delhi;* Stefan Nowotny Publishers

Wa Thiongo, N. (1981) *Decolonizing the Mind, Politics of Language in Africa*. New York; Heinemann

William, C. (1992) *Destruction of Black Civilization*; Chicago; Chicago University Press.

Mmap Nonfiction and Academic books

If you have enjoyed *I Can't Breathe and other Essays*, consider these other fine **Nonfiction and Academic books** from *Mwanaka Media and Publishing*:

Cultural Hybridity and Fixity by Andrew Nyongesa
Tintinnabulation of Literary Theory by Andrew Nyongesa
South Africa and United Nations Peacekeeping Offensive Operations by Antonio Garcia
A Case of Love and Hate by Chenjerai Mhondera
A Cat and Mouse Affair by Bruno Shora
The Scholarship Girl by Abigail George
The Gods Sleep Through It All by Wonder Guchu
PHENOMENOLOGY OF DECOLONIZING THE UNIVERSITY: Essays in the Contemporary Thoughts of Afrikology by Zvikomborero Kapuya
Africanization and Americanization Anthology Volume 1, Searching for Interracial, Interstitial, Intersectional and Interstates Meeting Spaces, Africa Vs North America by Tendai R Mwanaka
Africa, UK and Ireland: Writing Politics and Knowledge Production Vol 1 by Tendai R Mwanaka
Writing Language, Culture and Development, Africa Vs Asia Vol 1 by Tendai R Mwanaka, Wanjohi wa Makokha and Upal Deb
Zimbolicious: An Anthology of Zimbabwean Literature and Arts, Vol 3 by Tendai Mwanaka
Drawing Without Licence by Tendai R Mwanaka
Writing Grandmothers/ Escribiendo sobre nuestras raíces: Africa Vs Latin America Vol 2 by Tendai R Mwanaka and Felix Rodriguez

Nationalism: (Mis)Understanding   Donald Trump's Capitalism, Racism, Global Politics, International Trade and Media Wars, Africa Vs North America Vol 2 by Tendai R Mwanaka

It Is Not About Me: Diaries 2010-2011 by Tendai Rinos Mwanaka

Chitungwiza Mushamukuru: An Anthology from Zimbabwe's Biggest Ghetto Town by Tendai Rinos Mwanaka

The Day and the Dweller: A Study of the Emerald Tablets by Jonathan Thompson

Zimbolicious Anthology Vol 4: An Anthology of Zimbabwean Literature and Arts by Tendai Rinos Mwanaka and Jabulani Mzinyathi

Parks and Recreation by Abigail George

FAMILY LAW AND POLITICS WITH BIOLOGY AND ROYALTY IN AFRICA AND NORTH AMERICA by Peter Ateh-Afec Fossungo

Writing Robotics, Africa Vs Asia, Vol 2 by Tendai Rinos Mwanaka

Zimbolicious Anthology Vol 5: An Anthology of Zimbabwean Literature and Arts by Tendai R. Mwanaka

Love Notes: Everything is Love, An Anthology of Indigenous Languages of Africa and East Europe by Tendai R Mwanaka

Zimbolicious Anthology Vol 6: An Anthology of Zimbabwean Literature and Arts by Tendai R. Mwanaka and Chenjerai Mhondera

BATTLING LANGUAGE RIGHTS GOVERNANCE IN AFRICA: SWISSELGIANISM, UBACKISM, AND THE AMBAZONIA-CAMEROUN WAR by Peter Ateh-Afec Fossungo

Otherness and Pathology: The Fragmented Self and Madness in Contemporary African Fiction by Andrew Nyongesa

Zimbabwe: The Urgency of Now by Tendai Rinos Mwanaka

Zimbabwe: The Blame Game, Recollected essays and Non-fictions by Tendai Rinos Mwanaka

The Trick is to Keep Breathing: Covid 19 Stories From African and North American Writers, Vol 3 by Tendai Rinos Mwanaka

Recentring Mother Earth by Andrew Nyongesa

Zimbabwe: Beyond Robert Mugabe by Tendai Rinos Mwanaka

Language, Thought, Art and Existence: New and Recollected Essays and Non Fictions by Tendai Rinos Mwanaka

Experimental Writing, Africa Vs Latin America Vol 1 by Tendai Rinos Mwanaka and Ricardo Felix Rodriguez

Fixing Earth Anthology: An anthology of Africa, UK and Ireland Writers, Vol 2 by Tendai Rinos Mwanaka

Africa Must Deal with Blats for Its True Decolonisation: Unclothed Truth about Internalised Internal Colonialism by Nkwazi N. Mhango

ROYAL BURIAL AND ENTHRONEMENT IN AMBAZONIA: INTERROGATING THE RELEVANCE OF POSTCOLONIAL EDUCATION IN AFRICA by Peter Ateh-Afec Fossungo

SCHOOL BASED HIV EDUCATION AFFECTING GIRLS IN SELECTED COUNTRIES IN SUB SAHARAN AFRICA by Ivainesu Charmaine Musa

HIV AND AIDS IN ZIMBABWE: A REVIEW ON THE RELATIONSHIP BETWEEN PERCEPTION OF MASCULINITY AMONGST UNMARRIED YOUNG MEN AND THEIR SEXUAL BEHAVIORS by Lucas Kudakwashe Muvhiringi

AFRICA'S CONTEMPORARY FOOD INSECURITY: SELF-INFLICTED WOUNDS THROUGH MODERN VENI VIDI VICI AND LAND GRABBING by Nkwazi Mhango

Upcoming

https://facebook.com/MwanakaMediaAndPublishing/

www.ingramcontent.com/pod-product-compliance
Lightning Source LLC
Chambersburg PA
CBHW070346270326
41926CB00017B/4004